COLD

HARD

TRUTH

ON BUSINESS, MONEY & LIFE

KEVIN O'LEARY

 DOUBLEDAY CANADA

Doubleday Canada and colophon are registered trademarks

LIBRARY AND ARCHIVES CANADA CATALOGUING IN PUBLICATION
O'Leary, Kevin
    Cold hard truth : on business, money & life / Kevin O'Leary.
Issued also in electronic format.
ISBN 978-0-385-67174-3
    1. Success in business. 2. Entrepreneurship. 3. Business enterprises.
4. Industrial management. I. Title.

HD62.7.O43 2011   658   C2011-902508-6

Photo Credits:
Page 6, 177, 193 Courtesy of CBC. Photographer: Marayna Dickinson, Alace Photos
Page 159 Courtesy of CBC. Photographer: Jeff Kirk
Page 167 Courtesy of CBC. Photographer: Roy Timm
Page 170, 174, 179, 199 Courtesy of CBC and 2waytraffic, a Sony Pictures Entertainment
    company © 2006. All Rights Reserved.
Page 189 Courtesy of CBC. Photographer: Carmen Cheung
Page 205 Courtesy of CBC. Photographer: Greg Paupst
Page 215 and 218 © Michael Ansell/American Broadcasting Companies, Inc.

Cover photograph: CBC, Greg Paupst
Cover design: Terri Nimmo
Printed and bound in the USA

Published in Canada by Doubleday Canada,
a division of Random House of Canada Limited

Visit Random House of Canada Limited's website: www.randomhouse.ca

10 9 8 7 6 5 4 3 2 1

AUTHOR'S NOTE

This book is the story of my money, and the personal journey I went on to make it. None of the content, anecdotes, stories, advice or recollections contained in this book should be construed as investment advice, especially as they relate to any financial products I may represent. Investors should speak with their financial advisors for any investment advice and to discuss the risks of investing in any financial product. This book represents my personal opinions and should be enjoyed as such.

—Kevin O'Leary

I dedicate this book to the loving memory of my mother,
Georgette, who led an extraordinary life and remains
an inspiration to anyone she touched during her time.
If there is a heaven, God has his hands full with her there.

CONTENTS

THE COLD, HARD TRUTH
ABOUT MONEY

THINK THE WAY MONEY THINKS

I'm going to give you the bad news first: we live in difficult times. The average person works harder than ever and makes less money than his or her parents. The markets are increasingly unpredictable and volatile. Making, keeping, and growing money feels like a harsh and precarious science. The average investor has grown wary and cynical, accustomed to blurry messages and exaggeration, baffled by banks, angry at CEOs, exhausted by the economic highs and lows of the last few years. Wall Street's reputation is badly bruised, many of its leaders led away in handcuffs or fallen so far from grace they've become untouchables. Esteemed investment houses have been brought to their knees by scandal and bad practices. Many banks and blue-chip corporations, the axes around which capitalism once revolved, have survived only because of massive government bailouts. Investors are increasingly reluctant to hand over hard-earned money to fast talkers making big promises. We've created an economy where small businesses are afraid to take risks because big businesses have taken far too many.

Here's the good news: amid all of this uncertainty beats the heart of the true capitalist, the entrepreneur who sees adversity as opportunity and carves a confident path through the financial rubble. More than governments, these trailblazers are the true paramedics of the ailing global economy. And I am one of them. I believe that as long as people like me are earning money and creating wealth, capitalism has a fighting chance. If what I'm talking about interests you, if you're reading this and thinking, "That's me!" or "That's who I want to be," I'm here to tell you how to get there. I can't tell you that building wealth is easy, but it is possible, and entirely worth it. Capitalism creates freedom, after all, and I can't think of a loftier, more important calling than that.

I'm known for my roles as a venture capitalist on *Dragons' Den* in Canada and *Shark Tank* in the United States. I'm also a financial analyst on *The Lang & O'Leary Exchange* and CBC News. Because of those privileges, I've developed a reputation for delivering the cold, hard truth to entrepreneurs and politicians who've squandered hundreds of thousands, if not millions, of dollars on bad ideas or policies. I'm often called the Mean One, the one to be feared, even the Voldemort of Capitalism. You might think these words hurt my feelings, that I would be insulted or angry. Not so. I have learned one of capitalism's most important rules: money may go to bad people, but it *never* goes to bad ideas. That's why people who think making money is a matter of "really wanting it" or "trying really hard to visualize the opportunity" always crash and burn. The only way to make money is to get completely honest about what money is. Think of money like gravity. It is a law, an absolute. You can argue all you want about how you *feel* about gravity. But when you're hanging off a cliff, do those feelings matter?

Some people also think that making money is a matter of being good or right. But money doesn't care about any of that. It also doesn't care about you or your family or your country. This is not necessarily a bad thing. Money is neutral. Money goes only where it knows it'll be safe, and that's generally in the vicinity of more money. So building wealth requires the ability to think the way money thinks, which means never confusing money with emotion. In fact, feelings are often obstacles to wealth, because feelings, like the weather, are mercurial, unreliable, difficult to pin down, and ever-changing. Money deals strictly with fact. And as money's biggest fan, I have learned a lot from watching how it behaves, where it goes, what it runs screaming from. When I speak the truth about money, I'm almost speaking *as* money. That's why I come across as harsh, mean, and brutal. I'm just channeling money, in my attempt to help you understand it and amass it.

WHATEVER YOU PAY ATTENTION TO GROWS

If you've picked up this book, it's probably because you're interested in understanding money—how to make it, how to grow it. Or maybe you want to know how to spot a good investment, or how to sell your product, or how to run your business or perfect your pitch. Maybe you want to figure out whether entrepreneurship is for you at all. This book addresses all of those things. It's also the story of my money, and how I took a few thousand dollars and turned them into billion-dollar businesses. In these pages, I'm sharing with you life-changing moments and the powerful lessons that have shaped my business philosophy. Along the way, I'll provide succinct summaries of those lessons and some questions designed to get you thinking about your own financial goals and dreams. Not everyone wants to be an entrepreneur, or to start and grow a business. But one thing's for certain: everyone wants to be financially successful and to make more money. I'll share my simple, clear-cut philosophy for investing, growing wealth, and becoming financially secure. I'll also tell you exactly how I built my fortune. You'll meet my mother, who taught me how to manage money; my father, who showed me how to sell anything; my stepfather, who taught me the difference between a dream and a calling; my teachers, who taught me how to turn weaknesses into strengths; my bosses, who taught me that I'd never be happy working for someone else; my partners, who taught me that in order to create wealth, I needed to pair up with people whose strengths compensated for my weaknesses.

With the guidance and commitment of all of these mentors, I survived a personal and professional journey that at times was harrowing, heartbreaking, but always thrilling and invigorating. In fact, I not only survived but thrived. If adversity has added energy and vitality to my game, triumph has made me immune to my critics. It's of no value to me to pay attention to naysayers, skeptics, or finger-pointers, because I believe *whatever you pay attention to grows*. Pay attention to the critics, and you absorb that negativity into your DNA, which infects whatever you're working on. Money will flee that inhospitable environment. Pay attention to the horizon line, keep your path uncluttered, tune out unnecessary noise, guard your precious time, and money will take root and thrive.

I'm not talking about ignoring constructive criticism, which adds value if it helps solve problems. I have a lot of time for good advice. What I'm talking about is ignoring the people who said that I couldn't get through school because I had dyslexia; that I would have to work for someone else to be successful; that I would never finish university, let alone my MBA; that I couldn't grow a billion-dollar business out of my basement; and that I couldn't sell investors on the idea that buying and holding on to stocks made good sense and would be tremendously popular. When I proposed this idea to banks in September 2008, they laughed at me. That, dear reader, was more than $1.5 billion ago.

I've made mistakes, inched close to bankruptcy, been sued, fired, and slandered. I've despaired about making payroll and have taken some detours that were ill advised. These are experiences I'll share with you in this book, because when you've stared down that black pit of financial failure and have found the strength to leap over it to the security of the other side, it gives depth to your experience. I take pride in the fact that all my new ventures began as small businesses and became million- and billion-dollar successes. I'll retrace the steps of that path, and along the way, I'll share some essential business truths that have helped me turn those ventures into fortunes. As any entrepreneur will tell you, the road to riches is never straight and narrow. It can be riddled with financial land mines. Too many times, I've watched entrepreneurs make common and costly mistakes that jeopardize their company's health and their family's security. I'll show you how to avoid those pitfalls and how to have a competitive edge.

Today, millions of dollars move through O'Leary Funds. This money belongs to people who trust me—and my team. I remain keenly aware of this privilege—all day, every day, from the moment I wake up to the minute I go to bed. I measure my success by asking myself some very simple questions: Did I go to bed richer than when I woke up? Did I help my investors do the same? What can I do better, or differently, tomorrow? And if O'Leary Funds decline, and my investors lose money, that bothers me to no end. I lose sleep. It's painful. But that's what I love the most about money. There is no gray zone. You either make money or lose it; you have it or you don't. When I hear a CEO casually shrugging off a financial loss, blaming the vicissitudes of the market, it infuriates me. Because here's the ultimate truth about money: even though it doesn't care about me or you, to make money requires us to care deeply about it.

CHAPTER ONE

SPEND THE INTEREST, NEVER THE PRINCIPAL— AND OTHER LESSONS MY MOTHER TAUGHT ME

WHY A$$HOLES GET RICH

It was the fall of 2006, and the place was Pearson International Airport in Toronto. I was with my wife, Linda, and our kids, Savannah and Trevor. We had just flown in from our place in Boston to hit the Toronto International Film Festival. I had to use the men's room, so I asked my family to wait outside for a second. While washing my hands and minding my own business, I could sense next to me a stranger turning and staring at my profile. He was doing it every few seconds.

These were the early days of *Dragons' Den*. If you tuned in to the CBC show back then, you'd have seen five well-dressed venture capitalists shifting around uncomfortably in mismatched chairs in some anonymous warehouse in downtown Toronto. The cast that first season consisted of Jim Treliving, of Boston

Pizza fame; Robert Herjavec, who made a fortune in Internet security software; Laurence Lewin, who had an enviable job helming a lingerie empire; and Jennifer Woods, a whip-smart cattle mogul. One after the other, jittery entrepreneurs descended a staircase to present their business proposals, in hopes of scoring much-needed injections of capital to take them to the next level. Much like in the real world, we invested in some, but we dismissed most. I have to admit that on more than one occasion during the shoot, I thought I had made a mistake aligning myself with this strange TV show that had originated, naturally, in Japan.

Back then, the pitchers were corralled in a hot tent in the middle of an industrial pit in downtown Toronto. We were fed bad food, worked long hours, and, frankly, were less than impressed with the quality of business ideas being brought to us. I'd seen the British version of *Dragons' Den*, which by then was heading into its second successful season, but I wasn't sure that a show about venture capitalism would really take off in Canada. I find the world of venture capitalism to be the most exciting arena known to man. But it's also full of dry jargon, where you bat around terms such as ROI (return on investment), EBITDA (earnings before interest, taxes, depreciation, and amortization), and valuation (what you think your company's worth). Riveting stuff to my ilk. But I worried that producers would have to cut out the business essentials in order to make a show like this palatable to the average viewer, thereby alienating its core audience of business fans.

We debuted on October 3, 2006, to lackluster ratings—a disappointment, but not a surprise. Every week, however, the ratings seemed to creep up a bit. By the end of season one, we were a cult hit—by no means as big as we are now, but people had begun to tune in. I started to become recognized in public, at first in the business arena, and then at the odd restaurant or function, and now I was being gawked at in an airport washroom!

Finally, I shot the guy a look, as though to say, "Do you mind?" And there it was, that flicker of recognition.

"Hey," this stranger asked, "are you Kevin O'Leary? From that TV show *Dragons' Den?*"

"Yes, I am."

"I love that show!"

"Thank you."

"But *you* are a total asshole."

"Oh, really?" I said, a little shocked by such an insult. "Why do you say that?"

"Because you and those other Dragons stole that company from those kids last night. Asking for 50 percent. It's outrageous! You completely stole their company and their souls."

He was talking about a company called JobLoft, created by three savvy MBA students. They had built an easily navigable website that advertised minimum-wage jobs in restaurants and other franchises. I, and a few other Dragons, leapt on it. During the pitch, Jim Treliving alluded to the increasing difficulty in finding restaurant workers for that high-turnover industry, and here was a website that corralled them. (The deal fell apart during the check handover, in a spectacular storm of post–due diligence hubris. More on that in chapter 9.)

"Wait a minute," I said to the irate guy in the bathroom. "Those kids built a great website, but they've never run a business. We have every right to want control. That's what you do when you get into business with novices who've never made a dime.

They'll learn a lot from us. And that knowledge, my friend, doesn't come free."

"Still," the guy said, throwing his spent paper towel in the garbage can, "you're an asshole."

"Maybe so," I said, "but assholes get rich because they're not afraid to ask for what they want."

The gentleman left in a huff. He saw a woman standing outside the washroom.

"Guess who's in there," he said as he passed her. "That asshole Kevin O'Leary from *Dragons' Den*."

"Yes," the woman said, smiling wearily. "I know."

That woman was Linda, my wife.

Since that incident, I have been called much worse names than "asshole"—on and off the screen. And I'll tell you why it has never bothered me: because I speak the truth. Not just because I'm a nice guy and want to do the right thing, both of which are mostly true. I tell the truth because I don't like to lead people astray or to waste time. Money's great, money's the point of everything, and I can always earn more. But time is a scarce commodity. It is the true universal currency, because you can't invent, manufacture, or buy time. And not a day goes by when I don't lament that fact. Therefore, I have no time for people, places, or things that waste it.

A few months ago, I received a pitch from a smart-sounding sales guy about launching O'Leary Funds in India. It was an interesting proposition, but midway through the conversation, obstacles began to surface in my mind. As this man was speaking, I realized that the hurdles we'd have to overcome were too high at this juncture in our company's growth cycle. There'd be no way to structure the funds so that they'd get the kind of yield that

O'Leary Funds investors were accustomed to. I interrupted the pitch and told the sales guy that, for now, expanding into India was not a viable plan. But thanks anyway. He asked me if we could still book lunch, if only to lay the groundwork for a possible future collaboration. I said no, we wouldn't be meeting for lunch. He implored me. I said no again. There was an uncomfortable pause. Instead of calling me an asshole, which is what I think was on the tip of his tongue, he thanked me and got off the phone. I had clearly hurt his feelings. But my only thought was, "Oh well." Unless there's money to be earned, I don't take meetings with people I don't know or need to see. That hour of lunch went into a precious "time bank" I guard as fiercely as I would a few bars of gold. You might say that this man could have become a valuable contact, someone I could eventually do business with. Maybe. But instead of spending my time on more remote possibilities, I prefer to spend it on current ventures I know will yield results. That's why I said no. It's not personal. I call myself the Merchant of Truth because I speak the truth to everybody all the time. And it can sound blunt to the unaccustomed ear. It might make me come across as an asshole, but that's only because the brutal truth is so rarely spoken these days. It's like an ancient tribal language we've forgotten we know how to speak. But it's a language I learned at the feet of a woman who was a master with money: my mother, Georgette.

NEVER LET THEM SEE YOU SWEAT . . .
AND NEVER PAY WITH CREDIT

I was born in Montreal, Canada, in 1954, smack dab in the middle of the baby-boom generation, about as statistically average as you can get. But nothing about my family was average. On my mother's side, I'm descended from a long line of Lebanese merchants, who passed down that vital Phoenician blood. The Phoenicians were merchant mariners—traders and sailors—who basically put a price tag on one-half of the Mediterranean, selling it to the other half. Silk, tin, wood, or textiles—it didn't matter as long as they could make a buck. That Phoenician facility with money, coupled with my biological father's Irish charisma and gift of the gab—a laboratory couldn't blend a better vintage of salesman DNA than mine. Business is bred in my bones.

In 1904, my maternal grandfather, Joseph Bookalam, came to Canada from a small village in Lebanon. He was sixteen, and he headed straight to the mining town of Cobalt, Ontario, where he had an uncle who owned a general store. He worked like a dog for about three years, running the till, handling the inventory, and serving customers. Finally, he'd saved enough money to buy a horse and sleigh, and he struck out on his own. Like his forebears and his progeny, he couldn't stand working for someone else, so he became a roving salesman, trading with indigenous populations that dotted the outlying villages. Like a true Phoenician,

My grandfather Joseph Bookalam in 1941.

he didn't care who his clients were; he had no issues with their religion, ethnicity, or race. If you wanted what he had, he'd sell it to you: cooking and hunting utensils, supplies for the fur trade, all of it for cash. The man didn't do credit.

While visiting relatives in the States, he met my grandmother Akaber and proposed immediately. (Coincidentally, they were from the same village in Lebanon. Only in North America can two people who've never met in their small Lebanese village meet and mate!) They moved to Montreal, where they raised four children. Eventually, with his considerable savings, he opened Kiddies Togs, a factory that made high-end children's winter clothes.

At its height, Kiddies Togs employed dozens of people, and my grandparents did so well that they were able to afford a second home in Ste. Adèle, Quebec. My grandmother was a natural inventor, and she designed the system that brought water to the house using gravity and the existing watershed. Pretty impressive stuff. They had money, but my grandfather was frugal and so strict that my mother risked her life one night rather than face his scolding. It was a terrifying incident that has become a part of our family folklore.

My mother was about twenty and had borrowed her father's car to go to a party. Around midnight, after dropping off the last of her friends, she stopped at a red light. Suddenly, a man jumped into the front seat and held a gun to her head, ordering her to keep driving. My mother didn't scream, didn't panic. She followed his instructions, which were to keep driving in no particular direction. After a while, she finally took a good look at her abductor and realized this fearsome gunman was actually a malnourished, scared, and exhausted young man. Maybe he was a drug addict—it's hard to say. He was certainly desperate. Eventually, he asked Georgette to surrender the car. She was quiet for a few seconds, and then simply replied, "I can't do that. If I don't bring the car home, my father will kill me. And I think I'd rather you do it than him." That was not the answer he was looking for.

My mother then began a conversation with the man.

"What could be so wrong with your life," she asked, "that you would think this is the answer?" The man didn't reply. She began wearing down his resolve and dissipating his anger by telling him that if he killed her, he would ruin not only his own life and hers, but her father's, too, because he would die of heartbreak. My mother always had a way with lost souls. Not necessarily ones with guns, but still, people rarely ruffled her feathers. Along an abandoned street, the gunman motioned for her to pull over, fished out forty dollars from her wallet, and left. My mother drove home slowly, her nerves, which had been steely and calm, dissolved into shakes and shudders. By the time she got home, she could barely feel her legs.

She never told her father about the incident, never wanted to worry him unnecessarily. But it highlights one of her best

My mother, Georgette, as a young girl on a trip to Europe, *circa* 1948. This is my favorite picture of her.

qualities—her incredible capacity to remain cool under intense pressure. I have inherited some of that ability, though I would never want it tested in that particular way. But that skill, of never letting anyone see the roiling anxiety below the surface of a calm demeanor, would come in handy a few years later, when my grandfather died, leaving

Georgette, at the tender age of twenty-four, and her older sister, Edna, in charge of the entire Kiddies Togs operation.

MONEY = FREEDOM

In 1945, my grandfather died of a sudden heart attack. His only son, Norman, was seventeen, way too young to helm the company, so the task of running Kiddies Togs fell on the shoulders of my mother and her sister. They had logged quite a few hours in the design department, cutting patterns and doing odd jobs. But they had no idea how to run the accounting, purchasing, and marketing departments. So they had to learn those skills from scratch. How? Through trial and error, and by asking a lot of questions. The business flourished under Georgette's trademark pragmatism. She developed a real talent for managing money—in particular, for avoiding unnecessary debt. In fact, my mother always believed that debt was the source of almost every problem known to man. To her, debt was like a cancer, and if you didn't stay on top of it, it could completely consume you.

The first thing my mother did once she started earning a regular wage was to open up her own bank account with only her name on it. (It's the same bank account she kept her whole life, through two husbands, a few continents, and several countries.) Having her own money meant she'd always have her freedom. As an accidental CEO, she started studying the markets and interest rates, and over the years built a nest egg that, on more than one occasion, steered us clear of desperate straits and, frankly, helped me build my own empire. She also began investing in bonds. Georgette's philosophy: never spend the principal, just the interest. She would only invest in stocks that paid a dividend or interest. As far as she was concerned, a stock without a dividend was pure speculation. To this day, her advice guides me. It's the bedrock upon which O'Leary Funds is based.

Money and how you made it was never a mysterious subject to me. I remember very early conversations with my mother. I would ask, "Can I have some money to buy candy?" And my mother would say, "What did you do to earn it?" I learned early on that money didn't come from wishes and prayers. It came from hard work. Even at the age of four or five, I was aware that there was a direct correlation between work and money. She also taught me that you needed to leave money alone if you wanted it to grow. You should always save a third of your paycheck, investing it in stable stocks or bonds that pay dividends or interest. You spend that—never the principal.

Terry O'Leary marries my mother, Georgette Bookalam, in Montreal on November 3, 1951.

"That way," she said, "you'll always have money. And if you always have money, you always have freedom."

In handing over her philosophy on money, my mother was also explaining to me how the whole world worked. I began to understand that money is the lifeblood of a family. Love may be its heart, but it's money that pumps the vital energy through it. She treated money with respect, and when she needed funds, they were there.

Soon after taking over the business, my mother realized that she needed one hell of a sales guy to differentiate Kiddies Togs' superior quality from other children's apparel lines that were being manufactured overseas. My mother hired a charismatic Irish extrovert named Terry O'Leary as her head salesman because he had the qualities she lacked. Where my mother was pragmatic, Terry was spontaneous. Where she was careful, he was extravagant. In the beginning, it was a good partnership, in which one's strengths mitigated the other's weaknesses. They

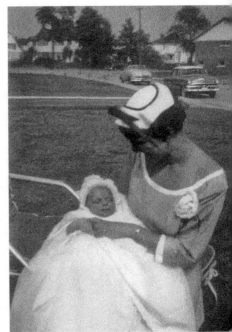

Born Terence Thomas Kevin O'Leary, July 9, 1954, in Montreal.

soon fell in love and married, in 1951, had me in 1954 and my brother, Shane, two years later.

You can easily see why my mother fell for my father, Terry. Here was this happy-go-lucky, charming Irish guy, arriving in the midst of all her hard-working, dedicated seriousness. He must have been a breath of fresh air. But he drank, played cards, and caroused—three things that dramatically clashed with my mother's value system. It wasn't a lifestyle she had in mind for herself or her children. But if it was an unhappy marriage in those early days, we didn't know it. My mother did an incredible job of insulating Shane and me from the fights that eventually erupted over my dad's behavior. All the while, she kept her money separate—some of it, we would later learn, earmarked for an exit strategy.

In the Lebanese culture, businesses get passed down through the sons, so my mother's younger brother bought out his sisters and eventually took over Kiddies Togs. It did well for decades, but with manufacturing increasingly moving to China and Southeast Asia, Kiddies Togs eventually sold for about $3 million in the early '80s. My mother was no heiress. Any money she had left was money she had long saved from the buyout and invested.

DON'T JUST READ THE ROOM—BE WHAT THE ROOM NEEDS

It soon became pretty clear that my parents' marriage was irreparable, and they eventually separated. When I was six, my father moved out and my mother was awarded full custody. It was a devastating, acrimonious split, but my mother did a masterful job of smoothing over the trauma.

My father would pick us up most Sundays, Shane and I clambering into the back seat of his long, dark car. He'd ask us about school; we'd tell him about our friends. Sometimes he'd take us fishing, or we'd grab dinner somewhere, usually a place where people knew him and were happy to see him. We were always overjoyed by his company, always fascinated by his stories of how he'd pull in big clients. He was still working for Kiddies Togs, so he'd regale us with plans to make it the most successful children's clothing company in the city, if not the country. The fact that he was a salesman was a huge point of pride for me. When I comb my memories of Kiddies Togs, a few things come to mind: the Coke machine that dispensed tiny, cold glass bottles; the sewing machines that were so loud you couldn't hear yourself talk; and the larger-than-life salesmen in the front office. They carried themselves like celebrities, my father among the most charismatic. They had big personalities and a lot of freedom in those days. They weren't tied down to their desks, and seemed to come and go as they pleased. The girls in the front office (it was always women) seemed happy to see them, and I loved the competitive spirit between the men (it was always men)—for clients, for commissions, and even for attention from their female colleagues. Because the success of the company depended on how much they could sell, their jobs felt heroic to me. Sitting in the Kiddies Togs lobby with a cold bottle of Coke in my hand, watching these men operate, I decided I wanted to be one of them.

I learned a lot from my dad—in particular, that good salespeople don't just have the ability to read the room; they become exactly what that room needs. An average day with my dad, I'd watch him interact with people—whether it was the waitress at the diner, the man in the parking booth, the guy in the tackle shop, a police officer, or a postal worker. I'd see him morph, modulating his body language and voice, blending into the feel of the conversation, seemingly able to connect to anybody and everybody.

"To sell products," he'd say, "people have to be able to relate not just to the product, but also to the person selling it."

Those lessons were ingrained in me, but unfortunately, my father's tragic streak ran deeper than his entrepreneurial talents.

WEAKNESS IS OFTEN THE FLIPSIDE OF STRENGTH

It was around this time that another troublesome fact began to surface: at six, I wasn't learning how to read along with the other kids, a source of incredible frustration for my mother and my teachers. It was horrifying to be singled out in class to sound out a word I couldn't recognize, especially because I could understand what the word meant. That white-hot shame of feeling dumb or slow left me paralyzed. I'd look at a piece of writing, and it was as though the letters had been smashed together into one big pile. I was good with numbers and counting, but the ability to read rows of letters, and to turn them into words, completely eluded me.

There was no word for dyslexia back then, but small pockets of expertise around this kind of learning disability were starting to pop up in certain academic communities. Coincidentally, Georgette discovered one of the best of these schools in Montreal. She grabbed my hand and we made a beeline for the twelfth floor of the Montreal Children's Hospital. Bad enough I had a hard time reading; having to go to a hospital to fix it was mortifying. That feeling disappeared at the sight of the bright blue trampoline in a room off the lobby.

In the burgeoning field of special education, this was a pioneering program. Led by Dr. Sam Rabinovitch and Dr. Margie Golick, it treated the whole child—body, mind, and soul. Part of my weekly treatment involved jumping up and down on a trampoline for several minutes so doctors could study my hand–eye coordination, balance, and how both sides of my body worked together. It was ridiculously fun, and since I was also restless and hyperactive, it was a genius approach to teaching a kid like me. With all that energy burned off, I could finally fully concentrate. It's a strategy that still works for me today. Though I've given up on the trampoline, I love nothing more than a predawn game of squash before a twelve-hour shooting day, much to the consternation of the producers of *Dragons' Den*. But I mitigate my late arrival in the makeup chair by giving pitchers on the show my full attention.

Georgette scratched her head at the nontraditional teaching methods they used at the Children's Hospital, which included flash cards and making funny sounds. Margie would say, "I don't know if it will help to make him a better reader, but it will make him a better kid."

Their philosophy was also pretty revolutionary. Up until I entered the program, I harbored an incredible amount of shame about my learning difficulties. So the first thing they did was help me understand that my brain was wired a little differently, taking away the stigma of my disability. The job of the doctors, Margie explained, was to map out how the wires in my head were connected so that we could figure out what I *could* do—and it turned out to be quite a lot. They discovered that since I had to develop coping skills to compensate for my weak reading, I was visually and verbally gifted. I could speak with clarity and tell great stories. I had a steel-trap memory and a facility with colors and numbers. Using mirrors, we also discovered that I could read backward and upside down. No wonder I took to photography at a young age and developed an eye for composition without ever having taken a class. I later learned that dyslexic did not mean dysfunctional. I kept company with some pretty amazing people: Andy Warhol, Ansel Adams, Leonardo da Vinci, not to mention Ted Turner, Henry Ford, and Richard Branson—dyslexics, one and all.

The learning program at the hospital was never dull, proving to me that you can make almost anything entertaining with a little ingenuity. In fact, it's a crime not to. Consider *Dragons' Den*. It might be a big hit in Canada, but it has tanked in countries that didn't understand the main rule: entertain! We proved venture capitalism could be a riveting spectator sport.

It's no exaggeration to say that enrolling in special education changed my life completely. To be told that my dyslexia had an upside shifted my perspective on myself and the world around me, and it left me with five very important principles that carried me through the rest of my education, all the way to my MBA and into my business life.

1. Stick it out through difficulties. You don't have to be perfect; you just have to finish.
2. Stand up for yourself.
3. Explain what you need, clearly.
4. Ask questions.
5. If you don't understand the answer, ask for a better, clearer explanation.

Margie gave me this list, reminding me again and again that no one else would do those things for me. I had to do them for myself. All of these skills would come in handy as I changed schools almost every other year, but they've also become invaluable business tools.

That's an incredible legacy for an upstart teaching program on the twelfth floor of a downtown hospital. Margie went on to become an education consultant for the CBC and *Sesame Street*, and she published a popular series of flash cards for parents to help their children develop better reading skills.

Margie uncovered my entrepreneurial powers—chief among them turning weaknesses into strengths. For the first time in my life, I looked forward to attending class. The dyslexia felt less like an awful disability and more like a series of skills that my brain had been developing all this time to compensate for its deficits. Today, I don't worry about my weaknesses. I identify them, and if I can't fix them, I hire people to fill the gaps they create. Business operations, for instance, require an intensely methodical approach, strict organizational skills, adherence to certain protocols, and the ability to pay close attention to details. These are not my strengths, but if I want to run a successful business, my operations department has to be airtight, transparent, and efficient. So I hire the best operations managers in the business. I pay these perfectionists well, and they, in turn, keep me fully apprised of the ins and outs and ups and downs of every single aspect of my businesses.

Like a blind person with a great sense of smell, I made friends with numbers. They never betrayed or confused me, which is why I think dyslexics make great entrepreneurs. If you must compensate for your weaknesses, you often have to come up with some pretty creative solutions.

There is a lot of shame when children are told over and over they can't do something. These children rarely grow up to be success stories. Margie Golick removed that shame at the exact right time in my life, before it took root and hampered me, and for that I'll be forever grateful. I hope everyone finds his or her Margie.

BIG PERSONALITIES = BIG SUCCESS
OR BIG PROBLEMS

My dad's drinking went from troubling to alarming, and our weekly visits became an increasingly erratic event. He managed to still work and make money, but my mother was worried about our safety in his care. Meanwhile, through her family, my mother had met a young Egyptian man named George Kanawaty. He was doing his Ph.D. in business at the University of Illinois in Champaign-Urbana, after which he'd join the UN's International Labour Organization. We liked George, and it was obvious that he adored my mother. After they married, she packed us up and moved us down to Illinois, where George had rented a house on a suburban golf course. It was a jarring change from Montreal, but we were young and adaptable. Shane and I quickly made friends with kids on the street. In the summer, we watched a handful of them set up lemonade stands along the curbs. They gave passersby cups of lemonade, and the passersby gave the kids money. Incredible. How hard could it be to set up my own stand? And since I didn't pay for the product (Mom bought the juice), the capital (George set up the table and chairs), the salary (Shane was six; he worked for free), or the overhead (our yard), it was probably the most succulent profit margin I've ever enjoyed. But I stumbled upon a far better business plan by looking out the back windows rather than the front ones. Our backyard faced the tenth hole of the golf course. I watched as parched players stopped, rested their bags, and wiped their sweaty brows under the hot sun.

It would be eight more holes before they could grab a cold beer or soda in the clubhouse. I realized it was a perfect location for *my* lemonade stand, far better than the street, which, frankly, was becoming a saturated market. Operating a tenth-hole lemonade stand was like shooting ducks in a pond. I bled my competitors' profits dry, too, because by the time prospective customers hit the sidewalk after a round of golf, they were no longer parched. Even at the age of eight, I was not only earning money, I was crippling the competition, because I was instinctually aware that location was everything when it comes to retail.

Champaign, Illinois, was not only where I opened my first retail concern, it's also where I made my first television appearance. Shane and I were devoted to a kids' show called *Sheriff Sid's Corral* on WCIA, the local TV station. One day, George made arrangements for us to appear in the studio audience, a highlight of my childhood. I remember watching Sheriff Sid wander around the studio with his microphone to chat with shy kids near the front. Then, all decked out in his cowboy costume, he approached me. I can't remember what we talked about, but we engaged in a full-on five-minute chat. (What can I say? Maybe I gave good sound bites even back then.)

My first television appearance: on *Sheriff Sid's Corral* in Champaign-Urbana, Illinois, in 1962, when I was eight years old. That's me on the right and Shane on the left.

Meanwhile, my father, Terry, was increasingly frustrated by the distance and his inability to see us when he wanted to. Eventually, frustration turned to fury, and one day he called and told my mother to pack our things; he was coming down to Illinois to bring us back to Montreal. Instead of waiting around for his knock on the door, my mother fled with us to Switzerland. The plan was to lie low in Europe until George and Terry could somehow reach an amicable solution.

We bought tickets to Paris under assumed names. From there, we took a train to Lausanne, Switzerland. Georgette must have been desperate to keep us away from my father, who by then had fallen in with a very eclectic crowd, real Montreal characters. She didn't want us to be raised in that environment. Today I can say without a doubt she did the right thing, but back then it was such an unthinkable action—a mother essentially kidnapping her children so they in turn would not be kidnapped by their father. But our tense situation soon turned tragic.

On October 27, less than two months into our exile in Switzerland, we received the news that Terry had died suddenly, in Montreal, probably of a heart attack. Shane and I cried when my mother gently broke the news to us. My father's body was shipped to Ireland for burial. Shane has since visited his gravesite to say a proper goodbye. I'm planning to do the same one day.

As a boy, I was heartbroken by my father's death. As a man, I now understand that Terry was a lesson in the dangers of excess, and how easy it can be for a good man—a talented man—to go off the rails at a young age. I have seen what the sales lifestyle can do to the best of people: the constant travel, the potential for rejection at every turn, the need to manage money that comes to you in fits and starts. It's tough—not for the faint of heart. And though I love sales, and I love the life, I consider myself lucky to have been able to pull back from the precipice over which my father fell. By the time I became a salesman myself, I had shaken off a lot of the potentially harmful lifestyle choices that might have contributed to my father's early demise.

My birth father in 1954, in Montreal, during a night on the town. I know I have inherited many of his traits, both good and bad. He died when he was only thirty-seven.

DO YOU HAVE WHAT IT TAKES
TO MAKE THE SALE?

Sales often attracts extreme personalities, people who don't need a lot of security, who live by wits and will from deal to deal. The best salespeople know how to navigate the ups and downs of that kind of lifestyle. I know good salespeople when I meet them. Here are five key qualities great salespeople possess:

1. **They occupy the ground they walk on as if they had something to do with it being there.** It's all in the walk. My father, Terry, had "the walk." You could call it a strut, but that man made an entrance even if he was just walking into the bathroom. The posture, the poise, the skip in the step—it's all part of the way the best salespeople carry themselves, as if they're the keeper of the best secret in the world and they're here to share it with one lucky customer. Great salespeople bring a vibrant energy into every room they enter. The icing on the cake is the way they dress—sharp, tailored, something that they've likely spent some coin on, and if not an expensive haircut, one that looks like the stylist paid close attention. A good rule of thumb is to dress like the people you're selling to: Don't wear a three-piece suit if you're hawking artisanal beer at a chain of pubs. And I'd whack any employee who showed up in a T-shirt to sell million-dollar mutual funds.

2. **They know a little bit about everything, but a lot about whatever it is they're selling.** Margie Golick taught me way back that as a dyslexic, I *should* have my hand up in every classroom; she showed me how to get comfortable asking a lot of questions. And I tell my sales staff that if their clients have questions they can't answer, they'd better find someone who can. I'm never too proud to admit that I don't understand something, because it speaks less to my ability to absorb something and more to the other person's inability to explain it.

3. **The best salespeople are tenacious without being irritating.** You'll hear me say "Never take no for an answer" throughout this book. In those circumstances, I'm talking about the first no, the knee-jerk no, the no that hasn't been backed by research or a second opinion. I don't confuse go-getters with gadflies—those you bat away, who keep returning for more punishment. If your prospect isn't interested, don't waste time convincing him or her. Chances are a reluctant client will be a problematic client. Besides, there are plenty more who will want to hear about what you're selling, so spend your valuable time finding them.

4. **Great salespeople aren't nice—but they are kind.** There's a big difference. I don't like nice. I don't trust nice people, but I find kindness very attractive. Nice salespeople will say whatever it is they think you want to hear to make the sale. And they do it in the sweetest way possible. Kind ones tell the truth. They don't sell false promises. They don't use flattery to butter up clients. And they most certainly don't

inflate, exaggerate, or misrepresent their product, company, or service.

5. **Great salespeople like themselves and love what they sell.** I can't call it anything else but joy, but that's what they emanate. Maybe that's why I love being around salespeople who dig their jobs. The best ones give off a *joie de vivre*, because they understand the fundamental role they play in the great game: they satisfy human desires. Like a sports agent who haunts the semi-pro leagues, I pride myself on my ability to spot and recruit great sales talent. The best are worth their weight in gold, and if they make me money, they're richly rewarded.

CHAPTER TWO

YOU'RE NEVER TOO YOUNG (OR OLD) TO UNDERSTAND MONEY

MONEY IS MORE POWERFUL THAN ANY INSTITUTION

George's first posting was with the UN's International Labour Organization in Cambodia. My stepfather's job was to train local managers from various banks and trading companies on how to improve their productivity. It was during Prince Sihanouk's reign, before all hell broke loose in Vietnam, while Cambodia was still putting on the face of neutrality. It was an exciting time to live there, and looking back, I can now see how much I was able to absorb. I had no way of knowing at nine years old that these early years spent globe-hopping would profoundly shape my politics and influence my investment style, but they did.

We arrived in December 1963, Georgette holding a box of Christmas decorations, determined to bring a bit of home with us.

We enrolled in the French school at first, but my brother and I didn't understand a word of the language and begged my mother for days to pull us out. My reading was still stunted, and I had trouble keeping up. My brand of dyslexia also had the alarming side effect of completely throwing me off spatially. I could be walking down the street, and I would suddenly, for a few moments, have no idea where I was. The trick was to squeeze my eyes shut, wait, and continue when my coordinates kicked in. Shane and I desperately wanted to go to the American school with the other English-speaking kids. Today, we both regret that we didn't stick it out. Speaking French would have helped me later, when we acquired companies with offices in France. But we wore my mother down.

Phnom Penh was chaotic and beautiful; the streets were clogged with bicycles, scooters, a few cars, and tricycle taxis called cyclos.

Shane and I used to go with our cook to the crowded market to buy fruits and vegetables, and my mother characteristically began to throw herself into the culture, learning how to use the spices and speak the language. We blended in, we didn't live apart—a travel style I still maintain today. Don't get me wrong: I do dine in the finest restaurants and I like to stay in the best hotels. But if I'm sussing out an investment on the other side of the world, I love nothing more than taking a

My brother, stepfather, and me visiting the Michelin rubber plantations in Cambodia in 1964.

black-market cab to some underground noodle hut in the middle of nowhere because a local manager suggested it. It's the best way to really see how a country functions, and to glean hints about what direction its economy is heading in.

When we lived in Cambodia, I didn't fully grasp what George was doing there, but my parents' conversations were laced with words like *currency, economies, employment,* and *foreign policy,* notions that all wove in and around my Phoenician DNA, forming a sense of global market connectedness. My parents didn't dumb any of it down. I understood early on that one country's demise could be another country's opportunity. I was also given an impressive education in basic economics. George would take us to see the Michelin rubber-tree plantations, where we'd meet the managers and workers. While George held my hand, I'd listen to discussions about streamlining operations and updating finances. We'd spend the day in fishing centers like Kep and Sihanoukville, and I'd play with local kids while George talked to their parents about getting the cost of production down. At the time, you had to fly over dense forests to get to the ancient city of Angkor. There was only one decent hotel in the region, and even it had no air-conditioning. Today, that same region is a buzzing hub of tourism, with dozens of excellent hotels and restaurants. I have some money working in the region because I can chart the evidence of a country coming of age and an economy that continues to mature.

Our stint in Cambodia came to a difficult end. The Vietnam War was heating up, and the country was becoming increasingly isolated and the streets growing dangerous for Westerners. George's work was now completely hampered by political instability, and it became obvious we had to leave. Talking to George now about those years is very instructive. Here was a country, sparsely populated, where people did not have to work hard to live. Rice grew almost by itself. Fish was abundant, the landscape lush with trees and vegetation. Was productivity even a priority? Not once had the prince or any minister alluded to its necessity. In fact, during that first month in the country, before my mother and brother and I had arrived, George counted twenty-two days of holidays. Productivity was just not top of mind, and one man and a band of well-meaning labor experts could do little to change it. Following the Vietnam War, Cambodia was plunged into political and economic turmoil.

Today, the country is becoming an increasingly stable economic powerhouse, and it's not due to international programs. It's from the flood of cold, hard cash into the region, including mine. Communist regimes do not thrive alongside rapid economic growth, and if people have the choice between making money and marching in the mud, they'll choose money every time. That's why I'm hard on government agencies that have really great vision, that dazzle with their good intentions, but have no ability to execute their plans. Nobody in those days wanted to help Cambodia become an economic powerhouse more than George, and yet it would have taken superhuman powers for him to achieve any meaningful change in that country.

We took the long way home from Phnom Penh, stopping in Hong Kong, Tokyo, Kyoto, Honolulu, Los Angeles, San Francisco, Vancouver, and finally Montreal, where we stayed for six months until George received his next assignment: Cyprus.

DON'T LET OTHERS DETERMINE YOUR WORTH

I loved Cyprus. We lived in a small villa surrounded by grapes, citrus, and pomegranates—olive trees grew in the distance. My mother planted roses. We were stationed in Nicosia and spent summers in Kyrenia, renting a little house along the cobblestoned harbor, diving into the crystal-clear waters near the Crusader castle. It was a kid's paradise, and it's still one of my favorite places on the planet.

George's job in Cyprus, again, was to help businesses increase productivity, and I remember visiting cheese factories and construction companies, my parents making fast friends with people they kept in touch with for decades. It was around this time that George moved from being our favorite uncle to a real father figure, eventually becoming one of my most trusted advisers in business and life. But Cyprus was also the site of my biggest heartbreaks as a child; I experienced my first rejection there, and later, it became the cause of my first abandonment, or so it seemed to me at the time.

Me (left) and my brother, Shane (right), at the British Junior School in Nicosia, Cyprus.

Years later, in 2002, my brother and I revisited our school in Nicosia.

At the British Junior School, Shane and I fit right in and made a lot of friends. But there was one girl in particular whom I had a massive crush on. She was American, with long blonde hair, blue eyes, and an arrogant jerk of a brother. Kids don't keep secrets about crushes, and pretty soon she caught wind that I liked her. I was arrogant enough to think that now that she knew, it was only a matter of time before she was my girlfriend. So I was more than a little crushed when she started to ignore me, and devastated when I later found out why. It seemed her brother didn't think I was good enough for her.

"My sister can do *much* better than you, O'Leary," he sneered.

"Why? What do you mean by that?" I was genuinely stunned.

"You're just not *our* type of person."

Heartbroken and humiliated, I took the long way home. I was also confused. I didn't know what that meant: to be considered

Me, my mother, and Shane, at the Nicosia airport, Cyprus, in 1967—haircuts heavily influenced by the Beatles!

not good enough for someone. I had never felt that way before. I had never felt less than, not enough. Truth is, I had never been rejected like that before.

At home, I became sullen and my mother pushed me to tell her what was bugging me. Reluctantly, I repeated what the girl's brother had said to me. When I was finished, she lit up in indignation.

"Never let anyone ever speak to you like that again. Do you hear me?" she said, her finger inches from my face. "No one is better than any other person, do you understand? It isn't even possible." She also told me a person couldn't make you feel less than good enough without your permission.

"So don't let him make you feel that way. You have control over that."

Georgette never lied to me, so I believed her and held on to that lesson. Since then, I've been impervious to mean-spirited attacks, believing them to say more about my critics than they do about me. And since then, no accomplishment or achievement has felt out of the range of my abilities. I have never felt less than or better than anyone, in any company, no matter where I am in the world.

Soon after that humiliating episode, I asked out the American girl's best friend, Anne. She became my first real girlfriend, and we had a blast picnicking on the beach, diving for shells, hiking in the olive groves. Every time I hear the Beach Boys song "Good Vibrations," I think of Cyprus and my mother's wise advice. To this day, I don't even remember the American girl's name.

"NO" MEANS NEGOTIATE

In 1967, I graduated from junior school, and we packed to get ready to go to Canada for a few weeks in the summer, as we always did.

Knowing that the entrance exams for the only English high school were taking place while we were abroad, my mother asked the headmaster to allow me to write the test sooner. I remember studying for it, but I don't remember being worried. I wasn't pulling A's, by any means, but I wasn't the slowest in the class, either.

We were all stunned when my marks came back. I had failed the test—failed so badly that I was denied entrance into the only English high school on the island. It was a major devastation—topped off with a bit of that leftover shame from my early learning struggles.

My parents were in shock, in particular my mother. George had at least another year in Cyprus, and Shane was still in junior school. But the high school was implacable: No marks. No admission. No education. We headed to Canada with heavy hearts, knowing that I wasn't going to be returning with my family to this island paradise.

My mother researched schools in Canada, and found one in the Eastern Townships of Quebec, a military college called Stanstead, that was willing to take me on short notice. We were a tight-knit family, terribly close and loving. For them to go back to Cyprus without me seemed unthinkable, but it was the only solution. My mother remained behind for several weeks to help get me settled, staying in the nearby town. Every Sunday night, she took me out to dinner, dropping me off at the school after dark. Those goodbyes were torture. Even contemplating them today can bring tears to my eyes and raise a lump in my throat. Then came the final goodbye, which would take her from me for months. I'm sure she had to convince herself that I'd be okay. I'm sure I told her that I was okay. But things were never really okay at Stanstead.

I was thirteen, and it would be a long time before I could appreciate how beautiful Stanstead's campus was, with its red-brick colonial buildings surrounded by the Laurentian Mountains on the border of Quebec and Vermont. I couldn't see any of that as an angry, homesick kid. It would also be years before I could appreciate the education I got there, which, though strict, did prepare me for university and beyond. I learned to fend for myself and had an incredible amount of independence. I certainly grew up fast. But if Cyprus had an environmental, emotional, and cultural opposite, it was Stanstead. We were a dozen boys per room, stacked on bunks, side by side, in narrow, chilly dorms. Mornings began hours before the sun came up. I looked forward to the dances, when girls would be bused in, but even they couldn't wait to leave Stanstead. I got along, made friends, some of whom I still keep in touch with, but it wasn't a warm, friendly place. And I think being alone toughened me in both good and bad ways.

Later, George was transferred to Ethiopia, then Tunisia, and during school breaks, I would be so eager to visit my family at their new postings. One summer, in Addis Ababa, we attended some kind of formal ceremony for Emperor Haile Selassie. He was a larger-than-life messianic figure. I'll never forget the sight of him, surrounded by leashed lions, throwing wads of money into the worshipful crowds. It was strange and exotic — but then again, anything would be compared to a boarding school in Quebec. After those visits, it was always physically painful to leave my family. There had been some discussions about taking me out of Stanstead and putting me into schools in Tunisia and Ethiopia, but that would have only further disrupted my education.

39

Years later, the headmaster of the Cyprus school admitted to my parents that a group of students applying after me took the same admissions test I had, and they all flunked, too. That's when the school realized the test was too difficult and lowered the admission standards. The headmaster said it had been a mistake to reject me based on that single examination rather than waiting to compare my results with those of my peers. You know, one of my most glaring characteristics (for good or bad) is my reluctance to take no for an answer. The traumatic experience of being separated from my family at such a young age because of one failed test has a lot to do with that.

Fooling around in the middle of winter in my second year at the University of Waterloo, where I was majoring in environmental studies, and shuffleboard at the local bars.

There is always a chance the other person's wrong. There is always a chance there's been a mistake, an error in judgment. To me, no is an invitation to negotiate, to prod, and to come to some sort of compromise.

Today, I'm sure Stanstead is a fine institution. In fact, I once spoke at a graduation ceremony, and the coed population seemed like a solid collection of the best and the brightest. But for me, those three years in that school were lonely and miserable. I did learn military discipline, not to mention how to smoke cigarettes, polish brass buckles, run in the rain, and shoot and kill someone lying down. So that's something.

MONEY GOES WHERE IT CAN MULTIPLY

One of the lasting legacies of these international postings was my parents' insistence on blending into any culture, rather than existing parallel to it. They learned what they could of the local languages, and reveled in the local cuisines and cultures. Shane and I were not typical diplomatic brats, frolicking behind high walls, separate from the country and the culture we lived in. We made friends with local children, learned their customs and idioms. My parents' social circle stretched wide, far beyond the small and sometimes incestuous confines of diplomatic circles. I was baptized Catholic; my mother and George attended Greek Orthodox services in Cyprus; we lit candles in Buddhist temples in Cambodia; we visited mosques in Cairo; we attended Sunday school in a Methodist church in Illinois; and today, I occasionally attend Anglican services. My parents didn't make these decisions consciously. It was just the way they were: open-minded, curious, and inclusive. I try to carry on their traditions, passing them down to my own children.

When I was young, I didn't see the benefits of my kinetic childhood, or of the discipline I received at Stanstead. Change was difficult, at times traumatic. But these early life experiences have made me adaptable and ready to face new challenges. While researching investments, I love visiting far-flung factories, traversing rickety roads that lead to modern coastal port lands, taking helicopters across frozen tundra to visit state-of-the-art energy projects, eating the local cuisine, and talking turkey with the managers. But I don't weigh in on the political, cultural, religious, or social aspects in countries housing my investments; money doesn't care about those things, so why should I? It's none of my business.

Money simply goes where it can multiply, and I go after the money—and, on occasion, excellent local cuisine.

I believe now that those experiences have granted me a kind of burnished wisdom, and they're coming back to me today with dividends. Literally. In 2008, I invested heavily in shipping after a trip to Limassol, Cyprus, where I saw boatyards booming with business. In Geneva, Switzerland, the global banking center where George lives today, I get the inside scoop on how that country interpreted the financial meltdown in North America and Europe. All the while, I'm keeping a keen eye on oil and natural gas deposits found under Cambodian territorial waters a few years ago. They plan to start drilling in 2011. I'll keep you posted.

MONEY'S GOOD—YOUR OWN MONEY'S BETTER

After my whirlwind of a childhood, we settled down as a family in Ottawa, so for the first time in three years, all four of us lived under one roof. Shane and I went to high school in Nepean, and I took a few odd jobs after school—the first, working for my girl-friend's father, who owned a fleet of garbage trucks. I was sixteen years old when I had my first steady job and earned my first buck, and let me tell you, it was an empowering moment. Staring at that money in my hands—my own money—was love at first sight.

My job was to wash down the garbage trucks. It was repugnant work, zipping into a full bodysuit and aiming a power hose at some of the vilest caked-on material ever known to man. When the hose didn't do the job, I had to get in there with a scraper and loosen the festering plaque coating the truck's insides. But I did the job with vigor, not because I was into it, but because I didn't want my girlfriend's dad to think I was a wimp. He paid minimum wage, about $2.25 an hour, but for the first time in my life, I felt the autonomy and freedom that comes with earning a paycheck. I loved that I could make decisions about how I wanted to spend or save my money, because it was *my* money. It wasn't an allowance that could vary depending on my behavior or how flush my parents were. This money was all mine, and it felt like someone had turned on a tap. I still remembered what my mother had said about spending the interest, not the principal. So I took a third of my paycheck and put it in the bank. Even then, I had the sense to put money to work. My mother had also taught me how bonds worked—incredibly fascinating to me as a teenager, the idea that a five-year bond that yielded 6 percent interest need only be left alone to grow; that money, by virtue of just *being* money, could accumulate and attract *more* money. That fact flowed straight into my veins. I don't know if that's how I began to understand how wealth is built, but the notion that there was such a thing as interest, a kind of reward for leaving money alone to do its job, left an indelible impression on me. So I saved, even as a teenager. And then I would take the interest and spend it— never diminishing my principal.

EVERYONE SERVES SOMEONE

During the last two years of high school, I held a few odd jobs. I was a bricklayer for a while, and then I planted trees in suburban Ottawa. Then came the brutal and humiliating job that taught me where real power lies. I also like to think of it as the place where my entrepreneurial streak was fully revealed to me, where I learned that I was born to work for myself.

I applied for a job at Magoo's Ice Cream Parlour because I noticed that girls tended to gather in the Lincoln Fields mall after school, and that's where Magoo's was located. It was a cheery place, with pumped-in music, green walls, and Mexican tile floors. The boss was a bit witchy, but working there would be a surefire way to meet girls.

The first day went well. The boss gave me a general overview of the store and a clear outline of my duties, which included standing behind the counter, serving ice cream, and being friendly to customers. My scoop skills were sound, I believe, and I could say with pride that although it was a busy day and I was new, I kept the lineups short and the customers happy. Cone after cone after cone, I was keeping pace. The boss, seemingly comfortable with my performance, spent most of the shift in the back room, doing her paperwork.

My second day on the job was busier, but I was getting faster. During a lull in the action, the boss came to the front of the store, looking for me. I'll admit I was hoping for a bit of praise, perhaps for being swift, efficient, and a fast learner. Instead, she said to me, "Kevin, there's some gum in the grout on the floor. I want you to get down on your hands and knees and scrape it out before anybody comes back in."

The request stopped me in my tracks. For a moment, I was speechless. Embarrassing to admit, but the first thing that crossed my mind was that if a pretty girl saw me doing that, she might not talk to me. The second thing that crossed my mind was that I didn't get hired to scrape gum.

"That's not my job," I said. "My job's to scoop ice cream."

Her features twisted into the meanest expression I'd ever seen on a face.

Next thing out of her mouth was "You're fired. Get out of my store."

I didn't even know what *fired* meant. I bolted for my bike, hot tears of rage stinging my cheeks as I cycled home.

My parents weren't impressed. My mother shook her head and left the room. My stepfather explained that in life and work, you have to serve something or someone.

"In this case," he explained, "you were hired not just to serve customers but to serve the person who owns the business, whether you like that person or not."

"Fine," I said. "I'll never work for anyone ever again. I'll just work for myself."

"Well, even if you're self-employed, you'll be serving someone," George said.

"Yeah, myself," I replied.

"No, Kevin. You'll be serving your clients or your customers. You'll never be successful if you think of work as serving only yourself."

It would take me years to under-stand what he meant by that, but he was right. Today, I am in business for myself, but I know whom I serve: I serve my shareholders, and I do it passionately and happily.

After the shame of being fired from the ice cream parlor subsided,

Me with George Kanawaty, my stepfather and one of my key advisers in business and life.

after the lectures about my insubordination died down, what remained was a dawning understanding that to be an employee was to allow another person to have a lot of control over my life. My boss held all of the power, because she could, for any reason, stanch the flow of money to me in an instant. I'll admit now that she had good reason to fire me. My moment of defiance was met with swift punishment. But I also realized right then that being an employee was not going to make me happy. To be happy, I would need to be in charge of my own destiny. I would need to become the boss, the purse-string holder, the one in control of the fate of the company. It wouldn't happen for a while, but I knew it would happen one day. Truthfully, it was as though an arm swept aside a heavy gauze, illuminating a clear entrepreneurial path.

WHO'S THE BOSS?

At the moment of my first firing, I received a message from deep inside of me, near the place that determined I'd be right-handed, around the corner from my dyslexia, and next door to the place that said I'd be bald by the time I was twenty-five. That message said, "Kevin, no more scraping the gum. You're not here to follow orders. You're here to give them. You're not an employee. You're an employer." This is a crucial lesson, one I ignored years later, much to my peril, after working for the company that bought mine for billions.

Lately, I've been thinking about my boss from Magoo's. If I could ever track her down, I'd write her a big, fat check, because she did me a great favor. She removed any notion that I could be happy working for someone else. I am an entrepreneur. I employ. She motivated me to want to finish school, to study, and to make something of myself. Today, I take a bit of comfort in the fact that I could buy and bulldoze the Lincoln Fields mall and sell it to Walmart for a tidy profit. But I digress . . .

I want to be clear here: I was not built to be an employee but that does not mean I am better than the people I employ. I'm different from them, but not better. In fact, if an employee of mine ever thwarted one of my directives, told me they didn't want to scrape the proverbial gum off the proverbial floor, I'd fire them. Pronto. I employ a lot of people who are very happy working for me. The ones who aren't happy reveal themselves pretty quickly, and I never hesitate to cut them loose. As George once told me, in business, as in politics, there are no permanent friends or permanent enemies; there are only permanent interests. And as long as my employees' interests align with mine, we'll be fine. The minute they don't, they're gone, whether I like them or not.

I'm telling you all of this for a reason. You must discover which role suits you best: employee or employer. Being a successful employee requires continually honing a talent for diplomacy and collaboration. You're rewarded with security and a steady salary, with fewer of the headaches from which entrepreneurs suffer. Running a successful business, on the other hand, is an all-consuming, all-encompassing venture, which totally invigorates some, totally exhausts others.

"EQ" TEST: ARE YOU AN EMPLOYEE OR AN EMPLOYER?

To determine your "EQ" (your Entrepreneurial Quotient), and to learn whether you've got what it takes to be a leader in business or industry, answer the following questions with one of these four options: *always true, quite true, rarely true,* or *hell, no.*

1. I need to know exactly what I'm going to make next year, and the year after that, and the year after that.

2. When I'm working on something, it has my full and complete attention, and I hate having that thought process interrupted by anything or anyone else. I'm a one-thing-at-a-time type of person.

3. When adrenaline's coursing through my veins because I've just made an aggressive offer on a competing company and I have yet to hear what the answer is, I feel incredibly uncomfortable and I have to lay down with a hot-water bottle on my tummy. I hate adrenaline.

4. There is nothing more gratifying than knowing that someone else takes care of automatically depositing my biweekly paycheck into my account. It gives me a warm feeling of safety and regularity, like a steaming cup of laxative tea.

5. I like the people I work with, and I hope none of them ever leave or move on. In fact, I hope we get to work together for the rest of our lives, always and forever.

6. I like that my work duties are very clearly spelled out, with no chance for ambiguity or spontaneity, and that nothing can be put on my desk to throw me off my daily, even hourly, routine.

7. If it's not in my job description, I don't do it—not because I'm lazy, but because it's someone else's job and I wouldn't want to offend them.

8. Sleep is incredibly important to me. In fact, I'm a grouchy little monster if I get less than my eight hours a night.

9. Work/life balance is so important. True success means a healthy amount of "me time," for long bubble baths and walks on the beach, or for enjoying hobbies such as pottery or ballroom dancing, which can be good for stress reduction. Oh, and spending quality time with my family. I don't like to miss any of Junior's hockey games.

10. I find living a life of extremes to be very stressful. The idea of being on a plane for twenty hours, or having people constantly need to speak to me, or being sought after for speaking engagements, or dealing with the ebb and flow of millions and millions of dollars—mine and other people's—seems like a nightmarish existence meted out as a form of punishment for something bad I might have done in another life.

If you answered *always true* or *quite true* to a majority of these questions, chances are the roller-coaster ride of entrepreneurship is not for you. There's nothing wrong with that. Believe me, the economy—indeed the world—would be much better off if people ill suited to running businesses would step aside and let those who are equipped take the reins. There's a certain kind of humility that comes from knowing where you fit in the economic stream. Compared to entrepreneurs, employees have a lot of freedom and a fraction of the stress. You can carve out a very healthy living working within the corporate structure and rising through its ranks. But that is not how you become incredibly wealthy.

If you answered *rarely true* or *hell, no* to the majority of these questions, get ready for the ride of your life. Deciding to become an entrepreneur is a lot like deciding to become an actor or writer. You're going to be constantly dissuaded by people who don't want to see you get hurt. They'll tell you the odds of succeeding are slim. They'll say that it's a hard life, full of anxiety and uncertainty. They'll remind you that you'll be spending nights and weekends either at the office or thinking that you should be there. And they'll be right. But if you *still* believe that there is no greater goal than working for yourself, creating jobs and opportunities for others, and being a player in your local, national, or global economy, then, like me, you probably have entrepreneurialism encoded in your DNA. You want to achieve the freedom money grants you.

To be an entrepreneur, you must find a business you can fall in love with. It has to be something you want to live, breathe, and eat. It has to force you to make compromises you wouldn't otherwise make. You know you've found it when, despite the fact that you eat on the run, rarely sleep, travel constantly, never see your family, and never relax, for some reason you've also never been happier.

CHAPTER THREE

TO BE OR TO DO:
THAT IS THE QUESTION

PUNKS DON'T GET RICH

Eighteen is a critical age. You hit a juncture that branches off into four clearly marked paths: professional, scholar, artist, or worker.

Take none of those paths, and you end up a punk. My arrow kept pointing in the artist direction. I had an artist's temperament, an artist's sensibility, and an artist's complete aversion to a nine-to-five life. Problem is, I loved money.

My dyslexia by then had faded into a mild impediment, and though words on the page were no longer jumbled, I never developed into an

That's me in high school in 1971 . . . and yes, that's my own hair.

enthusiastic student. And I liked to party. In other words, if you looked at a snapshot of me at that time, you didn't see a future captain of industry. I had no dreams of donning a suit and entering the workforce. I did, however, excel at art—photography in particular—and I rarely left home without a camera. I had a good eye and learned how to develop my own film. I loved spending hours in a darkroom, hanging my photos on a wire to dry. I wanted to pursue some kind of career in photography. I liked Francesco Scavullo's gig, shooting hot models for *Cosmopolitan* magazine covers. I thought I'd be good at that. Ansel Adams certainly had an interesting career, traveling the world, snapping stunning landscapes. I could do that, too. In my mind, since these men were successful and famous, I assumed they were wealthy. So I figured photography was a good way to make a living, and if my enthusiasm matched my talents, maybe I could also get rich.

My last two years of high school were a bit of a blur, much to my parents' consternation. After I crashed my mother's BMW, my future wasn't looking all that promising. There were four of us in the car when I ran a red light and was sideswiped by a cab. Miraculously, we all walked away without a scratch. The BMW, however, was a write-off. My mother was beyond disappointed; George was deeply worried. He later told me that during the years we lived in Ottawa—when

I crashed my mother's car in 1972; it was totaled, but amazingly, I wasn't hurt.

I was between about sixteen and nineteen years old—he and my mother rarely slept through the night.

The accident shook me to the core. If I continued down the path I was on, I'd end up dead—or worse, broke. If you're a teenager reading this because you see me on TV, maybe you're looking to me for some answers. Good. Pay close attention to this next sentence, because I'm going to tell you the first thing you have to do if you want to stay alive and be rich.

Here it is: Grow up.

Punks don't get rich. Even Mick Jagger's strut is just for the stage. I have it on good authority that the guy's a financial wizard, with an eye on every single penny that goes in and out of his multiple accounts. He's not rich because he's a Rolling Stone. For every wealthy Jagger, there's a broke Ramone. He's rich because he treated his money with respect. And he knew when it was time to put down the bong and pick up a prospectus. If you don't believe that

Just for the record, that's a cigarette. And just for the record, I quit years ago.

behind Justin Bieber's success is a vicious and calculating machine that exists to squeeze every conceivable dime out of the pretty little hitmaker and his rabid fans before his voice finally changes, you're sadly mistaken. And if you think Mr. Bieber's not in on it, put this book down and go back to pouting in your bedroom with your headphones on, because I can't help you.

But if you want to learn how to a make fortune, you've grown up enough to keep reading.

WHAT ARE YOU WILLING TO *DO* IN ORDER TO *BE*?

It came time to tell my parents about my plans for the future. We were a household that deeply valued education. Shane was making a beeline for engineering, an aspiration he had held since he was a kid. Me, they were still worried about. Success was not a given for me. I liked music, taking pictures, and hanging out with my friends.

In my last year of high school, George sat me down for the Talk About My Future. I was fidgeting, reluctant to pay attention, worried about telling him of my photography dreams. But George was adamant. His singular question: What do you want to *do* with your life?

I told him that I didn't want to go to university. That I was going to be a photographer.

"That's not what I asked you. What do you want to *do* with your life?"

I repeated my answer with greater conviction.

"Okay. That's all well and good, Kevin, but do you have any idea what you have to *do* in order to *be* a photographer?" he asked.

I didn't know how to answer that. Be? Do? There's a difference? I crossed my arms and mumbled something about taking night classes, getting an agent, opening a gallery. I had no idea what I was talking about, but it sounded good.

Then he asked another crucial question.

"How much money do you think you'd need to make, every year, to be happy?"

I told him $20,000, which in the early '70s was a lot of money. He shrugged.

"Most photographers don't make that much money," he said. "They'd be lucky to pull in a few thousand a year. On the side." He explained that the majority of my income would have to come from a job of some kind, a job I wouldn't necessarily *like* doing, but one that wouldn't interfere with what I *love* doing. That was the "do" part of George's question.

"Are you willing to *do* that—to work at a job in order to support yourself as you try to *be* a photographer? That's how it's done, Kevin. Actors wait tables between auditions, and writers hold down steady jobs, writing in their spare time."

What was I willing to do to make money while I honed my craft? Lay bricks? Work in retail? Clean garbage trucks? Plant trees? I'd done all those jobs. The idea of spending the rest of my life subsidizing a passion felt impossible, and because I had no postsecondary education, those were about the only jobs for which I was qualified. George wasn't discouraging me. He was being brutally honest about my chances at making it. Without the drive to work at other jobs to support that passion, I had no chance of becoming a wealthy photographer.

So "To be or not to be?" isn't the question. The question is: What are you willing to *do* in order to *be* what you want to be? It's not enough to say you want to be a photographer, or an actress, or a writer. You have to want to do all the necessary difficult things that are required to support that goal. Lots of people are willing to do just that. Some of them make it, both at the doing and the being. Most don't. I simply wasn't willing to take that risk, to perform all the tasks and jobs required to support my dream of becoming a full-time photographer. I wasn't willing to work days as a bricklayer or at a mall, shooting and developing photos at night and on weekends. I wasn't willing to cold-call newspapers or magazines, or to send them my unsolicited work. I didn't want to inch toward my twenties — maybe even my thirties — accumulating debt and rejection, just to build a portfolio of work or a string of shows where some or all of my photos would go unsold. There was no shame in understanding that about myself. It was an important, life-changing discovery. But it meant that I had to stay on the scholarly path, because getting off the path altogether wouldn't take me anywhere good. I wasn't willing to make artistic pursuits my full-time priority, and I really wouldn't have fared well as a punk. I love money too much.

IF YOU CAN'T MONETIZE A SKILL, IT'S A HOBBY

I waited until the last minute before I applied to a bunch of universities, but the only one that accepted me was the University of Waterloo. I decided to major in environmental studies because I love the earth and all its wonders . . . and it offered the easiest course load. I minored in psychology because I wanted to meet girls and that's the subject they were most interested in, probably to help them figure out boys. As a parting gift, when I left home to go to the campus, my mother gave me a used BMW. She was superstitious. Since I had survived that awful wreck, she figured this car would keep me safe. I had been saving up my money toward a down payment on a new car, but Georgette urged me not to incur any debt going into university.

My roommate was an out-of-control alcoholic, and within weeks of my bunking down with him, he got kicked out, so I had the dorm

In my hippie phase on the way to the University of Waterloo in the fall of 1974.

room all to myself. When I wasn't studying the earth and chasing girls, or shooting with my new camera, I was honing another natural talent: shuffleboard. I stumbled on this skill accidentally, and even more accidentally, I found a partner, Paul Chaput, who was good at the things I was bad at. He was excellent at hanging rocks off the far corners for maximum points. I was good at knocking out opponents straight on. We were a perfect team. We started placing bets—twelve bucks a game at the local pub. Winner takes all. Loser buys a round. We figured it was good to lose the first few rounds, because our opponents would get a bit hammered. Then, alert and on fire, we'd win the last few rounds. It was an excellent strategy. On a good night, we took home a couple hundred dollars—and there were a lot of good nights. I didn't need to get a part-time job. I was living off the proceeds of my shuffleboard wins. In fact, I could earn more playing in shuffleboard tournaments in and around the Kitchener-Waterloo area than some of my instructors made teaching. Paul and I made so much money that, one day, a local bar owner clamored for a cut of the winnings.

"After all, you're using my shuffleboard equipment to earn cash," she explained.

I was outraged.

"Forget it! We're bringing in loads of customers who spend a ton of money at your bar!"

"Too bad," she said. "If you don't give me 10 percent of the winnings, go play somewhere else."

She knew there were no other bars with excellent shuffleboards and a big enough space for spectators. She held us hostage, financially, and we paid. I resented her then; I admire her now. What a terrific lesson! We were on the weaker end of that deal. That's the difference between making money and creating wealth. Sure, we were making good money playing shuffleboard, but we weren't becoming wealthy. The bar owner, however, had just discovered another way for her existing business to generate more revenue without hiring anyone or building anything.

Getting rich doing what you're good at is just the first step. Good at playing pool? Become a pool shark. Love yoga? Get your teaching certificate. But despite all your commitment and energy, these qualifications alone won't make you rich. I learned that you have to own the pool hall or the yoga studio where you ply your passions. Then you're not only making money—you're building wealth. You're hiring people, opening franchises, and competing to conquer territories. That's what puts you in a real power position. *That's* how you grow wealth.

The other thing I began to understand was the true definition of partnership. I'm not talking about the ability to work closely with someone you get along well with. I don't care about getting along with people. That has no bearing on whether you're successful. I'm talking about finding a partner who has and does what you don't have and can't do. Those are the kinds of partnerships that have real value, and on my journey I've been lucky enough to have had a few stellar partners, without whom I wouldn't be where I am today. Paul and I won because we had completely different skill sets. Did we get along? Sure. But that's beside the point. Even if I hated him, I would have made it work because we were making the kind of money together that we couldn't have made apart—the hallmark of a great partnership.

Mostly, I understood that my true talent wasn't playing shuffleboard; it was *making money* from playing shuffleboard. My talent wasn't the skill itself; it was monetizing the skill, a lesson often missed by passionate people in pursuit of turning a hobby into a career. No matter how good you are at something, if you can't make money from it, it's a hobby and should remain so. Remember: it wasn't that I didn't love photography, but until I could figure out a way to monetize it, it remained a hobby. I learned all of these lessons years before the thought of entering an MBA program even crossed my mind.

Meanwhile, since I was out every night earning shuffleboard money, my marks began to suffer. In my final year of environmental studies, I was required to produce a thesis. The idea of sitting down and writing a long, turgid essay about some injustice committed against the planet by greedy humans did not appeal to me. So I used my fallback skill, photography, which had been expanded to include shooting movies. I produced and shot a documentary about the Grand River Conservation Authority's battle against the construction of a local dam. It was intended as a statement about the environmental havoc the dam would create in the region. Today, I would never produce that kind of propaganda, but it's a great example of how my passion began to dovetail with what would eventually be my first profession: film-making. I received the highest marks of my academic career for the documentary—so high the project elevated my average to near honors level, which helped get me into the MBA program at the University of Western Ontario, in London. When I started my undergraduate degree, I had no idea that I would want to pursue an MBA. But George convinced me it would give me a practical

set of skills. He called it a toolbox. The more skills I put in my toolbox, the greater my chances of success.

For my MBA thesis, I proposed to film something that would represent what I had learned over the course of my two years of study, with the added value that the school could use the film as a recruitment tool. From the money I earned playing shuffleboard, I hired Scott MacKenzie and Dave Toms to help me produce the documentary. The school administrators flipped for the idea, and the project

Working behind the camera directing a film about my first year in the Ivey MBA program in 1979. The film was used for years as a recruiting tool.

Graduating from the University of Waterloo in 1977 as Mom looks on with pride.

had a twofold impact: it set me apart from my peers by highlighting my skills, and it diminished the focus on my weaknesses by putting less emphasis on reading and writing. For two years, I interviewed students and teachers about their academic goals, following their progress during the course of the program. The film told the story of how you go about getting an MBA, what's taught, what's required, who does well, who does poorly, and why. I received very high marks.

The film had a major impact on my life. In fact, it saved me academically. I find it incredibly lucky that my ability to produce pictures stemmed from my inability to read words, and luckier still that a year later, I figured out a way to start a business monetizing those skills. I'm living proof that every weakness can be turned into a strength.

AN MBA MIGHT MAKE YOU SMARTER—BUT NOT MORE SUCCESSFUL

I'm often asked if I think pursuing an MBA is worth the expense. Think of Mark Zuckerberg of Facebook fame, who didn't even finish his undergraduate degree at Harvard, let alone get an MBA. Bill Gates is another college dropout. And though I wouldn't say I'm smarter because of a business degree, I will say it gave me a head start, and some needed discipline. Spending twenty-four months doing just one thing was extremely challenging, yet extremely necessary, because it helped develop my very limited attention span. It nourished a brain that needed to be pushed to its limits. I learned how to defend an idea, verbally, in front of a room full of people—another skill that wasn't in my personal toolbox. Before business school, I had a big mouth, but my opinions were unformed and often went unchallenged.

Most important, I made valuable contacts at Western. I don't remember a single thing about accounting, operations, or finance, but I would say that at least one-third of the members of my graduating class have become stinking rich, well connected, and ridiculously successful. They are the leading lights of capitalism, and they've spread their talents across the globe. Believe me, I graduated with one hell of a Rolodex. To this day, it's a handy thing to possess when I'm looking for an opportunity or an investment. I don't brag when I say I know the management of every bank in Canada, or that I know the head of AltaGas or every tech luminary from San Francisco to Switzerland. I can walk into a swanky restaurant in Boston or Geneva and know at least a handful of people by their first names, including the waiters. My calls get returned—a valuable thing if you're investing with my company.

An MBA might also get you an interesting placement right out of school, or a brief gig between your first and second years, but it's not going to set you up for life. And all those contacts I mentioned? Well, that works both ways. If they like you, maybe they'll hire you. If they don't like you, they won't—you'll be dead to them after graduation. I went to school with guys and gals who were brainiacs with the books, but utter zeros when it came to making money and building a business. They had no people skills and no ability to forge valuable relationships, proving that in the real world, inter-personal skills often trump academic achievements.

Over the course of my postsecondary education, I stuffed my toolbox with valuable skills. I learned how to make money from the things I was good at. I learned how to focus on my strengths and to deflect attention away from my weaknesses. I learned how to select and work with ideal partners. My psych studies provided a good base from which to study the greedy and opportunistic character traits of the average human being. Business training taught me how to monetize all that knowledge. Plus, I had a Rolodex worth the cost of tuition—not a waste of twenty-four months. But I still hadn't achieved a very important entrepreneurial goal: I still hadn't earned a dime for anyone else.

BE LIKE THE MAGPIE

In 1979, between the first and second years of my MBA program, I applied to a number of companies for a summer placement. I had to get some valuable corporate experience, and I was lucky enough to be picked for a four-month stint at Nabisco, the food giant headquartered in downtown Toronto.

There was no doubt in my mind that I would never be happy being an employee. But my goal at the time wasn't happiness—it was experience. En route to working for myself, I was fully aware I was going to have to work for other people from time to time.

The finance world has its bears and bulls, but I'd like you to consider another animal from which entrepreneurs can take their cues: the magpie, the ultimate bird-world entrepreneur. Magpies are considered aviary thieves. But I like to think of them as resourceful and persistent, using everything and anything they can gather to build and fatten their nests. Nothing goes to waste. And they're not picky. A piece of tinsel will do when a string's not available. The other thing I admire about the magpie is that it's one of the few creatures that can recognize itself in the mirror: this bird knows who it is—another important entrepreneurial trait.

I look back on the few times I worked for other people, before I built my own fortune, as my Magpie Years. Every lesson I learned, every mistake I made, every skill I honed, all went into lining the nest of my own experience.

DO WHATEVER IT TAKES TO GET THE ORDER

My job title at Nabisco was Assistant Brand Manager. My task: increase market share for their biggest cat food brand. I hate cats, but I loved the idea of getting their owners to spend more dough on them.

My first day, I took the streetcar from my place on Shaw Street to the twentieth floor of the North Tower of the Eaton Centre in downtown Toronto. Standing on the pavement that early-summer morning and looking up at that glass-and-concrete tower, I waited for that surge of pride, for that sense of possibility to well up inside me and overflow. Here I was, this dyslexic, good-for-nothing punk, now on the cusp of corporate greatness. Right? But that's not how I felt at all. The building looked like a giant ant colony, and I was just another ant. I was taken through the ant corridors and shown my ant pod, and the CEO came by and shook my ant hand. He was a talented guy who now heads a big food distribution network, and he was quite clear about my job.

"Sell more cat food, O'Leary. Grab more market share. Do it by inventing more flavors and whacking the ones that aren't selling. Go!"

Then he introduced me to the brand manager, and that was the last time I saw the CEO.

"Listen, kid," said the brand manager. "Do you have a strong stomach?"

I had survived Cambodian street soup. I had washed putrid ooze from the inside of a garbage truck. I told him I was the least queasy person he knew.

"Great. Time for you to see how we make cat food."

He took me to the rendering plant a few kilometers outside of Toronto. I'll never forget it. There were two cattle cars piled high with the remnants of animal carcasses already pilfered for the good stuff. Left over were the beef lips, beef sphincters, chicken giblets—stuff you wouldn't usually find on your dinner plate. Another car was piled with fish scales, fish bones, fish faces, fish tails, and fish bellies. The scraps were beyond animal. Dissected like this, they looked like alien body parts. Workers in full protective gear raked all of this flesh into two big vats of papaya juice. The unholy stew festered and boiled in room-sized witches' cauldrons. The room smelled like death and fear, with weird undertones of tropical fruit. It was nasty stuff.

After this animal detritus was reduced to two vats of beige and beiger paste, the juice was strained, leaving one vat labeled LIVER PASTE, the other SEA OF JAPAN. Using these two pastes, I had to increase market share by creating more flavors. My job wasn't to suggest a new paste base. These two were all I had to work with. I was to add ingredients in an endless array of combinations, give them new names, maybe new labels, creating new flavors to market.

It was a revelation: two pastes, endless flavors. To the liver base, I could add some starch and bullion and call it "Chicken and Rice." Add green peppers to the Sea of Japan paste, and I could call it "Salmon Delight." Add bacon bits to the liver paste: "Meat Medley." The possibilities were endless.

I lined up my new flavors and booked a sales conference at a hotel for the buyers. After my presentation, the group seemed enthusiastic. Then a senior buyer put up his hand.

"O'Leary, you *say* these new flavors are delicious, but how do we *know* that?"

"Because I said so." I had heard the rumors that brand managers had to actually eat the dog and cat foods they pitched, but I thought they were just that—rumors.

"Well, I'll give you the order, O'Leary, but I want you to eat the cat food. I want to see you enjoy it."

I looked over at my brand manager for help. He solemnly nodded, like a doctor delivering some very bad news. So in a conference room full of buyers, I scooped up the tragic paste, smeared it onto a slice of Melba toast, paused, then ate it with complete and total enthusiasm, licking my fingers for effect.

We got the orders. A few days later, the brand manager put in a request to hire me full time after I was finished my MBA. I imagined myself as part of this massive corporate machine. One year, I'd be selling cat food; the next, cat litter; then maybe chocolate, then crackers, then soup. There's a good living to be had selling that stuff. Maybe even a career. I tried to picture coming to work every day on the streetcar, lining up for hot dogs at noon outside of The Bay, hitting the Pickle Barrel for happy hour, and I just couldn't. It wasn't for me. Some people thrive in an environment with clear goals and targets. I saw in my colleagues that sense of satisfaction that came from purposefully climbing the corporate ladder. And marketing is an interesting science, one that still fascinates me. But I wanted to take bigger risks. Mostly, I wanted to make more money. A *lot* more. And I wanted to make it on my terms.

If you want to be an entrepreneur, know that there will be stretches of time when you will have to work for other people. But know, too, that there will come a time when you need to leave the nest. Here is what I suggest: give yourself a time limit as to how long you'll work for others. For me, the knowledge of a looming deadline came swiftly, almost on my first day, when I felt a general sense of unease, as though the work culture itself didn't suit me. You must set your own deadlines. Will you quit after you've made a certain amount of money? After you've amassed a number of months, or years, of experience? After reaching a certain job level? After making a certain number of contacts? After learning everything you can about the industry? Only you can decide what those deadlines are. Meanwhile, as you do your job, and do it well, gather everything shiny and useful and bring it back to your nest. (I'm not talking about stealing office supplies — you should get whacked for that. I'm talking about gathering skills, learning how an industry works, and figuring out what kind of team you'll need around you when the time comes to go out on your own.)

HOW TO SPOT WINNERS

One of the biggest lessons I learned in my first foray into the corporate world is that you're safe only as long as you're earning money for your company. You can be the savviest grad at your swanky school, but you're useless on the open market until you can prove your value as a moneymaker. When I lecture at schools today, I tell students that they're all "Nothing Burgers" until they earn cash for me. I tell them they have no intrinsic value until they earn *me* money first, then make it for themselves. That's how it works out there in the real world. They don't like to hear this. They want to believe they'll graduate into a gig with a $250,000 base salary and a company car. Many of them get a rude awakening. Here are five things I—and a lot of other employers out there—look for in prospective employees:

1. Proof you can make me money, by clearly showing me how much you made for my competitors. You have to assure me that you have a plan to secure new ways to generate even more money for me than you did for my competitors.

2. Willingness to travel far and wide, surviving (and thriving) for long periods of time away from family and friends. Regardless of our technological strides, money requires face time. As you'll read later, I learned that the hard way.

3. Unfailing honesty about your failures. Don't candy-coat screwups. Put them on the table. I'll find out about them

anyway, so you might as well fess up early. You should also demonstrate that you've learned your lessons from past mistakes, and that they won't happen again.

4.   An aura that sizzles like an isotope. Winners take on a certain electric glow; you know them when you see them. They have a certain lack of defensiveness. Combine that with a relaxed humility, and you get the sense that you just like being around these people.

5.   Your résumé's printed on crisp white paper with clean fonts, few pages, and even fewer fancy words. The more decorated and complicated the résumé, the more likely it is that I'll toss it in the trash. And though I like to see an MBA beside your name, I'll hire a moneymaker over a scholar any day.

CHAPTER FOUR

LOSE A PAYCHECK, GAIN A BUSINESS

KNOW WHEN TO GET IN—
AND OUT—OF A BUSINESS

My MBA film scored me some work as an assistant editor on a film about the Canadian men's Olympic volleyball team. I did some other gigs, pulling in a paycheck here and there, but I needed to have a stake in the business. Suddenly, it dawned on me: Why work for other people when I could generate TV work myself? I could finally answer George's question about what I wanted to do with my life. I wanted to be a filmmaker, and I was finally willing to do any of the jobs in that industry because I'd be doing it for my own bottom line. Plus, I loved the work. TV production seemed like the perfect meeting of the left and right sides of my brain. The work is fast-paced and creative. It requires you to think on your feet and operate on adrenaline. With luck, timing, and good marketing, TV work could be lucrative. I brought on board Scott MacKenzie and Dave Toms, the guys who'd worked with me on the volleyball film and helped shoot and write my MBA film. We called our company Special Event Television. As a sportswriter, Dave brought with him a lot of contacts in the industry, including the producers of *Hockey Night in Canada*. They approached him one day with an idea to make five-minute films to fill the second intermission on Saturday-night NHL games. We could produce anything we wanted, as long as it fit the time slot and the ideas were hockey-related. Working on 16-millimeter film with old recorders, we'd get the assignment on Monday and have the items shot, written, cut, and fed by Saturday. It didn't pay much at first, so to cover our bills we took other gigs, including producing summer catalogs for Canadian Tire. But we were having the time of our lives, traveling across the country and hanging around pro athletes. I could have been very happy making a good living in the television industry, but the money gods had other plans for me.

Special Event produced some very popular shows, including *The Original Six*, about the first key teams in the NHL, and *Bobby Orr and the Hockey Legends*.

Two of the three founding members of Special Event Television. The company started *Don Cherry's Grapevine*, *The Original Six*, and *Bobby Orr and the Hockey Legends*. I used proceeds from its sale to start SoftKey Software Products Inc. That's me, standing, and Scott MacKenzie, sitting in the middle, along with other colleagues.

The Gump Worsley Story was a short documentary about the iconic goalie who was one of the last to play without a mask and carried the scars of the game on his face with pride. However, the feather in our company's cap was a little show called *Don Cherry's Grapevine*, a half-hour interview program that aired on Hamilton's CHCH-TV. It starred the man who would go on to become the most outspoken former coach in hockey history.

Don Cherry was just emerging as a TV personality, wearing his outrageous clothes, his arm draped around his funny-looking bull terrier, Blue. We were feeding off his growing success, and with *Grapevine*, people were able to feel like they were getting even closer to him. Right before my eyes, and from behind my lens, I watched a charismatic man become a TV icon. Any time the camera was on him, he was on. He was a total natural and a pleasure to shoot. He abided by a few golden rules of television: 1) Never be boring. 2) Never be small — make every gesture big, dramatic, and bold. 3) Always be the antagonist, not the protagonist — being the good guy's not interesting. 4) Always, *always* get the first *and* last words.

You may not agree with what Don Cherry says (and by the way, he truly doesn't care), but as a viewer you always have a great time watching him. He is a masterful carnival barker, a hockey intellectual, and most important, he uses his opinions as a branding mechanism: he became the guy who brought the "brute" back to the NHL. Honestly, it never occurred to me that I would one day become a controversial TV personality, but I must have been taking a few notes.

Don Cherry's Grapevine became an incredible success for Special Event Television, and we drew in partners, including

Gerry Patterson, a hockey agent we were dealing with to secure access to players we interviewed. Gerry was a real philosopher. He used to say, "Put your head down, kid, and keep moving. No matter how bad it gets, all you can do is keep moving." Good advice for tough times, but Gerry was as ruthless as he was philosophical. We made money from the fact that we owned the formats of our shows, the most lucrative being *Don Cherry's Grapevine*. That show eventually got so successful it moved from CHCH to TSN. So it should have been no surprise to us that Gerry would at some point want a bigger piece of the pie.

One day, Gerry looked at the bunch of us and, out of the blue, said, "You know what I'm thinking? Why do I need you guys? I just need Dave, the writer. I can hire a shooter and an editor for a lot less than it costs me to keep the rest of you as partners."

Utterly ruthless—but totally right. He didn't need us. But what he didn't know at the time was that we also didn't need him—just some money. So the timing was kind of perfect. Even though I was reluctant to part with the company, when he offered to buy us out, we took the cash. I had plans for that money. Big plans. Buried in Gerry's buyout was another key lesson in business: if a company wants to buy yours, sell it, because their optimism often exceeds yours. That means they're willing to pay more than what the company's worth.

While building Special Event Television, I had begun dabbling in TV graphics, and in the course of perfecting that skill, I bought a personal computer and began to push the limits of what it could do for me. Soon I would partner with another man who would change the course of my business life entirely.

MONEY-MAKING IDEAS SOLVE PROBLEMS

We eventually sold Special Event Television. My share came to about $25,000, a small fortune that allowed me not only to put a down payment on a house on Shaw Street in Toronto, but also to go on to build a new business. An extraordinary one. The mark of a true entrepreneur is that when one venture folds or fails, you move on to another. You never stop. You never look back.

It was the fall of 1983. I was doing some freelance editing gigs, specializing in creating flashy title sequences. When you watch old TV shows, you can see how basic and rudimentary TV graphics were at the time. That's because they were shot on film, and graphics were a handmade, complicated process, involving stencils, rulers, layering, and lighting. Dissolving from shot to shot was an exacting task that took a very long time to get right.

The original Osborne "portable" personal computer, which ran a CPM operating system on which John Freeman wrote Keychart in 1984. Also pictured is an early version of a Keychart manual and floppy disks, which went on to sell millions of copies and launch the company.

I was also becoming increasingly intrigued by the world of personal computers and all that they were capable of. Very few people had a computer in their homes, but I had broken the bank on an Osborne PC that cost almost $2,000, a lot of money at the time. It had two floppy-disk drives and the WordStar word-processing program, and it ran the BASIC programming language, which I was just beginning to understand. It was portable, weighing only (!) twenty-five pounds, so I could take it with me on the road, show clients a design or a layout, get it approved, and lug it to the multi-pen plotters to duplicate and print out.

A plotter, which looks like a giant roller, is a machine that moves an ink pen slowly across a piece of paper, one line at a time — plotting out a larger version of the small design you create. It could draw anything, but a solid block of color could take hours to trace out. I used a lot of block letters to create TV titles, so you can imagine how cumbersome this process could be. Think of the difference between dot-matrix printers and their laser counterparts, then slow it down a few days. Except for architectural firms, which still need to use precision drawings for complex blueprints, room-sized plotters are obsolete these days, but they were a staple of my work back then.

A few months earlier, I had joined an Osborne computer users' group that met once a week in a downtown community center. (Yes, I was single. And yes, all of the members were men, and most wore short-sleeved dress shirts and pocket protectors.) We all had a deep and instant fascination with the personal computer and wanted to get together to swap information. It was a real-life chat room, if you will.

One night, I arrived late to the meeting. There were no seats left, so I stood at the back of the room, craning my neck to get a better look at what one of the geeks was demonstrating. He was John Freeman, an accountant at Suncor, an energy company. In his spare time he wrote computer programs, and he was midway through presenting some graphics software he'd just written. I truly couldn't believe my eyes. Imagine someone solving your biggest problem before you even thought it *was* a problem. John had created a printing program for titles and graphs, something he needed for his board presentations at Suncor. The software effectively took what he created in his computer and fed it directly to a plotter to print out, automatically. He could create charts, diagrams, and pie charts—everything you'd need for titles, slides, and presentations. No one had ever seen that before. I was beyond blown away. It was one of those magic moments when my brain, without my prompting, kicked in and knew exactly what to do with this product: make money. It was that automatic.

After the meeting, while the other geeks surrounded the computer to try the software, I cornered John, introduced myself, and asked him if he'd shown anyone else his product. He had run it by some work colleagues, he said, but that night was its public debut. He had a sense that plotter software would be useful to some people, but he had no idea what he had. He didn't know there was a massive global market for it. I told John he had invented a product that I wanted—*needed*—to buy, and if *I* did, so did hundreds of thousands of other people. Every designer in the country, every architect, everyone working in advertising, every editor, people in sales, marketing, television—you name it—needed this software. And I told him I knew how to get it in their hands. (I didn't, really. But I knew I'd figure that out later.) We formed a fifty-fifty partnership that night. He would create the software; I would market it.

That was the beginning of a very potent partnership, the perfect marriage between a creator and a seller. We were two young guys shaking hands in the cold, outside an anonymous downtown community center. We went on to make a fortune.

DROP THE FEAR, PICK UP THE PHONE

We met a few days later at our new headquarters: the basement of my house at 411 Shaw Street. The first order of business was a name. Microsoft was a growing monolith, having developed software that was included in most computers. We liked the word *soft*, and John threw out the idea that the plotter software was *key*, so we settled on the name SoftKey. Our first product—John's plotter software—was called KeyChart.

My first step was to pick up the phone and call plotter manufacturers. There was a lot of initial interest, but we were a one-product company. They all wanted to know what else we had, and the answer to that was nothing. The idea of establishing

Back where it all began, in the basement of 411 Shaw Street, Toronto, the birthplace of SoftKey Software.

distribution channels for a product like software was still in its embryonic stages. That's when it dawned on me that we could just copy what Microsoft was beginning to do: we'd try to bundle

our software with existing hardware. But instead of selling our software with computers, we'd ask the plotter manufacturers to bundle it with *their* existing hardware, since those distribution channels were harder to penetrate. Using leftover money from the sale of Special Event Television, I got on planes, then more planes, approaching as many plotter

When you're just starting out, you sleep at your desk. Luckily mine was in my basement.

manufacturers as I could: Hewlett-Packard, Watanabe, Tektronix, Epson, and Roland. The deal was this: they could license our software for pennies, as long as they shipped it out with every single plotter they sold.

So what did I do to get those meetings? I picked up the phone. Let me repeat that. I. Picked. Up. The. Phone. So many entrepreneurs with great ideas get stalled at this juncture. In fact, I shouldn't even call those types entrepreneurs. Too many great ideas die at the feet of those afraid to pick up the phone because they don't want to face potential rejection. And trust me, if you do take the risk of reaching out to venture capitalists and prominent executives, you will be rejected. Plenty of times. That's how entrepreneurial calluses are formed. For every ten or twenty executives who rejected my calls, there were two or three who took them. And they were the only people who mattered to me. You don't know who these people are until you find them.

LICENSING: *THEY* MAKE YOUR PRODUCT, *YOU* MAKE MONEY

I knew we had a terrific product only by instinct, only because this plotter software had solved a big problem for me and I was confident it could do the same for others. What John and I needed next was to find one company with the ability to include that software in their product. And we did: Enter Computers, a company operating out of San Diego. They agreed to sell the first version of our plotter software for their Sweet-P Model-100 "personal plotter." The price? A mere $800, a bargain back then. But it was the early '80s, and personal home computers were still like inground pools in terms of home luxuries. To have a personal plotter that could create professional-quality graphics was like having an adjoining hot tub with that pool.

John then reconfigured the KeyChart software to work not just with professional plotters but also with laser, ink-jet, and dot-matrix printers. Why shouldn't everyone be able to print professional-quality graphics for résumés and home businesses? That opened up our world and expanded our bottom line. Now our target market was every single *printer* manufacturer on the planet. I called HP again, then Epson, then Canon, and booked meeting after meeting. We were no longer just creating software that we licensed to plotter manufacturers for a few dollars — which then sold in the thousands. We now licensed our software for pennies because it was bundled with printers, which sold by the *millions*.

Licensing your idea to established companies to manufacture it is a beautiful business model—one I recommend all the time on *Dragons' Den*. Why bother with the headache of not only making your product but then distributing and marketing it as well? This presumes that your company has top-notch expertise in everything, and so often, that's not the case. Let an established business take what you've invented and put it through their manufacturing and distribution channels. Still, so many entrepreneurs remain unwilling to take a small fee in exchange for massive distribution. They balk at the idea, thinking they're being told their product is only worth pennies, forgetting that those pennies can quickly multiply into millions. They remain intent on manufacturing their beloved invention themselves, not realizing they'll have to elbow their way into the same distribution channels as their competitors. After that, they'll have to fight for shelf space, if they even get any. Then comes the most expensive part: competing for market share, which can erode a company's bottom line, jeopardizing its ability to continue to manufacture the product, let alone develop new ones. Not licensing your product is often a tragic business decision that can lead to a lot of casualties.

Here's an example. On the third season of *Dragons' Den*, a young father presented a clever portable camping trailer that he had invented himself. It stored your food, tents, and clothing and could be pulled behind a small car. We all liked the idea, until he explained his dream was to manufacture and sell the trailers himself. Robert Herjavec urged him to take it to a camper manufacturer, one with factories, skilled labor, and retail distribution channels already in place. Plus, we told him, the recreational industry might be looking for innovative ideas just like this. But no, he wanted several hundred thousand dollars to build the inventory himself—which wasn't even close to the capital he'd actually need for a venture this ambitious. He'd need millions, and I told him so. But he wouldn't budge, and eventually his idea died on the vine. You can see now why I get so impatient with this kind of limited thinking—because licensing means focusing on what you do best and partnering with others who have essential skills and knowledge that you lack. Licensing is precisely how I have made several product lines a success. Licensing is how I got rich.

ACT "AS IF" . . . UNTIL YOU ARE

Back at 411 Shaw Street, my avocado-green wall phone was ringing off the hook. We needed to sound like a growing company, so I hired a sharp woman named Mary Pat Lyons to help me grow the business, as well as a comrade from my MBA class, Gary Babcock. He was one of the best salesmen I've ever known. Since we were working out of an old Victorian house rather than a slick suite of offices, some subterfuge was required when we answered the phone. Mary Pat would say, "SoftKey Software Products," and she'd put callers "on hold" by covering the receiver with her hand and silently signaling me. I'd wait a few beats, then trot up to her. Phones were once connected to walls, so I went through a lot of cords, pacing and pulling. There was also no such thing as call waiting in those days. So I talked fast to prevent other potential clients from hearing a busy signal while I was tying up the line, which only made it sound like we were busier. John and I added "Suite 202" to the letterhead (my upstairs bedroom), because it sounded loftier . . . but that move almost landed me in some hot water.

Once, an executive from a Swedish plotter manufacturer flew into Toronto and said he wanted to visit our offices. Normally, we'd book a conference room at the airport, but he was insistent. I called Don Allen, a friend from my freelance editing days who owned an impressive-looking post-production facility downtown. I asked him for a big favor—to let me use his offices. Not only did he help me out, but he asked his staff to dress for the part! Normally, his staff—overnight editor types— wore their pajama bottoms to work, but on the day of our meeting, all our "staff" looked fantastically well groomed. Don printed up some professional-looking signs that said SOFTKEY and hung them throughout the offices. I had a limo meet the Swedish executive at the airport and bring him to "headquarters." At the last minute, just before our executive was about to arrive, Don spotted a young man with a giant head of rock-and-roll hair moseying his way down the hall. He took him by the shoulders, turned him around, and told him to go away and come back in an hour. Our presentation went off without a hitch, and we got the order we needed. Once SoftKey moved beyond the plotter stage into videos and graphics for CD-ROMs and DVDs, you better believe I threw a lot of work Don's way.

SoftKey was slowly becoming known in both the growing computer-geek realm and my burgeoning Bay Street circle. Most of the guys I graduated with in my MBA class were making names for themselves in the banks, investment houses, and brokerage firms, and these contacts would soon come in very, very handy. Everyone wanted to fund the next Microsoft, and I was one of the first conduits between the computer-geek world and the world of high finance. We used to throw insane parties at 411 Shaw. I'd invite half of my friends from Western, the other half from Bay Street and the computer club, and we'd round up as many women as possible. I bet a number of companies (and marriages) resulted from those parties. I sprung for another phone, the kind you could walk around with, though it was still tethered to the wall by an extra-long cord. In the morning, I'd hear it ring, then tug it out from beneath a pile of empty pizza boxes and beer cases.

I was living on Shaw when I met Linda Greer, a University of Toronto student who was working part time at the Toronto Squash Club. I liked her right away. But she wasn't remotely interested in me. I finally got up the nerve to ask her out, but she told me she had a boyfriend. I replied that I wasn't interested in taking her boyfriend out—just her. After a few persistent months, she finally buckled under the O'Leary Onslaught.

We were dating only a few weeks when I had to go out of town for a week. Mary Pat had also taken some time off, so even though Linda and I had only just started dating, she agreed to house-sit and answer the phone while I was away. I think that's when I knew Linda was "the one." Not because she was willing to answer the phone, but because she took me—and my burgeoning business—seriously, and nothing about my business fazed her.

We held our wedding party at the house on Shaw Street because we didn't have the money for a big reception. When we ran out of food, we ordered pizza. I got very lucky with Linda, because although I wasn't looking for someone who'd be a great mother, she turned out to be that, and more. For much of the next ten or so years, as the company grew rapidly, I was home less and less, and the responsibilities of parenting our two children fell more and more on Linda's shoulders. I was a good dad when I was around, but unfortunately, I wasn't around a lot. That's the price *all* successful entrepreneurs pay. I don't know one wealthy entrepreneur with a perfectly balanced personal life, who has attended every soccer game, who's a hands-on parent, sharing half the responsibilities. Especially as you grow a company, you have to live, breathe, and sleep your business. You have to dream about it, and when you're awake, you have to be daydreaming about it. If you want a family, forget about raising your kids. I hope you're as lucky as I was to find someone to hold down the fort while you're out being a provider. When it comes to parenting, that's about the only contribution I can brag about. The rest of the credit goes to Linda.

DON'T HAVE ONE INVESTOR LINED UP—
HAVE SEVERAL

SoftKey was a year old, with five employees and about $100,000 in sales. Not bad, but in order to grow we needed a fast injection of big money. I saw other companies around me that were getting money for nothing, for mere ideas, but we had a viable company with a few employees and a handful of software products, including KeyMailer, a program for managing mailing lists. It made writing corporate form letters easy by allowing you to paste a new address at the top of the same letter, over and over. But we had long since run out of Special Event Television money to use on SoftKey, and now we were running out of operating funds.

I came up with a number that would get us to the next level: $250,000. Then I called a friend of a friend from Harvard who ran an investment company in Toronto that was financing a lot of tech start-ups. After an aggressive pitch that included a film clip of me holding the future of SoftKey in my hands—shiny CD-ROMs that glinted in the sun—he said he'd be in for the quarter million. For that, he'd get a third of SoftKey. For the *Dragons' Den* fans who are reading this, we were valuing our company at around $750,000—a fair price, considering we had sales.

We hired a lawyer. Then we opened the champagne—prematurely, as we'd soon discover. The night before the investment came through, my prospect called me and pulled the plug. He gave no real reason. He just . . . changed his mind. At that moment, we were screwed. I had no backup plan, no other investors on the hook, no idea how to proceed. I'd poured my heart and soul into that one pitch for that firm, which turned out to be a very dumb mistake, one I have never made again. We came close to being sunk.

In our optimism, we had hired staff to support a potential growth spurt, and I now had no way of covering payroll. After the investor pulled out, I hung up the phone, punched open the front door on Shaw, and walked straight into the middle of the city. I didn't know where I was going or what I was going to do. Without cash, we'd be toast in a matter of weeks. How was I going to make payroll until we found new investors? How could I have left our company in such a vulnerable position? In high finance, things change in a second. People change their minds, due diligence uncovers a stench that was previously undetectable. Their dog dies, and suddenly they're in a bad mood. What looked like a great deal yesterday now looks like the worst idea on the planet. But I'll tell you what: I have never been caught out like that again.

Today, it's imperative for my companies to have at least four people on the hook for financing whenever I'm looking for investors. Lesson learned—the terrifying way.

I got home after dark and called the only person I knew who had $10,000 at her disposal: my mother. If I could make payroll for a couple of months, I knew I'd be able to score more sales, enough to stay afloat until we could take the company public. That was my next goal: an initial public offering. My mother wrote me a check, and we were in business for six more months. She was like that, my mother—not just with me, but with our whole family. She remained cautious and pragmatic with money throughout her entire life so that she could be generous when called upon. She saw money as energizing and palliative, and she had amassed enough in her own personal account that she could afford to use it to help others, something George always supported enthusiastically. Because they had shared a lifetime of careful money management, they enjoyed the two things—the only things, really—that money can give you: freedom and the ability to help others.

SCARCITY IS A GREAT TEACHER

I look back at that starving phase of our SoftKey start-up with a lot of fondness, despite the fact that my day-to-day life was intensely focused and mostly fueled by adrenaline and fear. When you're broke, you have to make vital decisions, decisions about which limb you really need. When you walk through the office, you start to see it through a very different lens. You begin asking questions that hadn't seemed so obvious weeks or months earlier, such as: Do we really need that guy? What does she *do* at that desk all day? How much am I paying her? Why? Can I find someone to do that job better and cheaper? Which office supplies are really necessary? Can't people buy their own pens? Can't we water our own plants? Why the hell do we even need plants? If you want shade or oxygen, go sit in the park!

When the stakes are high, you have to become ruthless about the bottom line—for your sake and for your employees' sake. When you're teetering on bankruptcy, you're never more clear-eyed about cutting and trimming, hiring and firing. But that's when you really come to understand the value of money, its flow in and out, where it thrives and where it disappears. Scarcity of cash is a great teacher. It's also good for camaraderie, believe it or not. Our early days looked a lot like the movie *The Social Network*. We were a bunch of men who slept in the clothes we wore to work that day; who lived, breathed, and ate our industry; and who partied with the same people we'd just spent all day

Taking SoftKey public—my first IPO (Initial Public Offering). That's Bob Rubinoff, lead director (left), me (middle), and Michael Perik.

working with—things few smart women would do to themselves deliberately. That's why it *was* mostly men. And they dominated the computer industry. (They still do, to some degree, though there's been some progress in the male–female ratio.) We worked that hard not just because we believed we were on the cusp of something new and great, but because we knew we'd make a pile of money if we stuck it out. Soon, it was time to go public. We needed money. But since we were still showing a loss, we couldn't list on the Toronto Stock Exchange. Luckily, the Vancouver Stock Exchange was ground zero for tech start-ups.

Back then, you could find securities companies willing to take an untested tech start-up public. If it failed, there were other tech companies right behind it. I was in a hotel room in Vancouver when SoftKey went public. The moment the first share traded and multiplied, I realized, "Wow, as the company's biggest shareholder, I'm now rich." I was a millionaire, at least on paper, and that lit a fire inside me that made me work even harder, because I now had shareholders who wanted to be rich along with me. Having shareholders is an incredible incentive to grow a company from a million in sales to a billion. Getting rich feels like joy. A hot burst in the heart. But when you realize you're also able to make *other* people rich, that's an almost indescribable high.

Going public also meant SoftKey's headquarters could move from my house on Shaw Street to offices on Richmond Street, in downtown Toronto, in the iconic CITY-TV building. They weren't fancy digs, but they were vast, and with ten thousand square feet of desks and people, we finally looked like we were worth a buck or two. The days of fake suites were over. No more putting the phone on fake hold. We had arrived.

Calling plotter manufacturers in the early days of SoftKey Software, *circa* 1985, on Richmond Street in Toronto.

These were the wild and woolly days of tech start-ups—the late '80s—when people broke the bank to buy computers and then acquired software one shiny, expensive program at a time. File sharing and the Internet were concepts still a decade away. Software was a retail push, and as I had proved with cat food, I knew something about retail marketing. So we started hiring sales support. But the industry was growing so fast, it wasn't uncommon for our sales team to also give technical support to a customer. We did whatever had to be done.

EVERYONE IS REPLACEABLE

In the beginning of every growing company, there's a hiring frenzy. I used to be so picky, such a perfectionist about who I brought into our precious stables. I'd scrutinize their résumés, interview them twice—three times—and call every reference they offered. I saw them coming with us on a long, long journey, and I was doing my due diligence to ensure a tight and functional team. Now I realize that very few people who are there in the beginning are going to be there at the end. I've also learned that if they're not going to work out, there's nothing you can do to fix it. The corporation's culture will emerge on its own, and the people who stick will settle into that culture naturally or will adjust to make themselves fit that culture. Anyone who fights against the company will eventually leave or get whacked. And though it's controversial to say this, it doesn't really matter who you hire in the beginning—most of them are going to leave or get whacked anyway.

So when do you whack someone? The moment you think, "Hey, this one's not really working out." The minute the notion enters my mind that I have to fire someone, I don't hesitate. I don't give the person three, four, five months to improve or change. Because I'll tell you something else that's unpopular to admit: problematic employees never change. I've made that mistake in the past, because gut-churning conflict is meant to be avoided. Right? Wrong. Dive right into conflict, because in the time that passes between realizing someone's wrong for your company and getting rid of that cancer, it's metastasized, spreading toxins far and wide. So I repeat: the minute you sense someone's not going to work out, let him or her go.

Who do I fire? The underperformers, the complainers, the players, the posers, the ones who infect otherwise healthy environments with their arrogance or their negative attitude or outlook. I get rid of them. I keep the process simple and respectful. There's always someone with me, usually from Human Resources. I take the troublesome, soon-to-be ex-employee into my office, politely sit the person down, and say, "Look, it's not working out here for you. I'm firing you. I don't want to go to war with you, or litigate, though I'm happy to take that on if I have to. So let's negotiate. Give me a number, one you think is fair, and we'll come to terms. I'll write you a severance check, and then I want you to pack your things and go."

Done.

You can use that script.

Many years ago, I fired a software salesperson who felt he had been passed over for a job and made a case to me that I shouldn't have gone outside of the company to fill the vacancy. He said he was perfect for that job. He said he was pissed I didn't pick him. The thing about sales is this: it's black and white. I pulled out his numbers and showed him the facts. He had been consistently underperforming. Not only that, there had been complaints within the company that he bruised morale. He was unhappy and brought everyone around him down, too. It's like a piece of sand in an oyster: that irritant is either coated or ejected. I ejected him. These days, in this economic environment, I don't tolerate sand in my oyster, because I don't have to. There are so many great people looking for work, I can blindly fish into a pile of résumés stacked to my right and yank out another winner. At the end of the day, the ugly truth is this: everyone is replaceable—including me, by the way. The only word I have for unhappy people who work for me is, "*Next!*"

As time passed and SoftKey became more successful, we started to attract high-quality staff. They saw our success and they wanted to be a part of it. We didn't even need to hire headhunters. We soon moved way beyond writing printer software to creating every kind of business and educational software imaginable: from dictionaries, to fonts, to spreadsheets, to encyclopedias, to math and taxes. If your small business, home office, or student needed software, we had it. We branded everything with the word *Key*, so there were KeyTimesheets, KeyTravel, and KeyMaps. You name it, we had it, and we sold our software for far less than our competitors.

Even the owners of the company sometimes have to slap on a nametag and hit the conference circuit.

We started to get orders faxed in from major distributors around the world. Every morning, a stack of orders thicker than a phone book greeted my assistant. Sometimes, the plastic in-tray would be so heavy it would snap, the faxes fluttering onto the floor. We were stamping millions of CD-ROMs, so many that one production run delayed the 1987 release of Michael Jackson's album *Bad* by four days. Record executives in New York went ballistic when they were told the album would be delayed. "What the hell is this SoftKey?" they asked. *Bad* went on to sell about eight million copies that year, which should give you some idea of how big we were, and how fast we were growing.

It was a new and expanding industry, so the talent pool of software writers multiplied every year. Those driven to make money flocked to us. They still do. Everyone who works for me is initiated the same way: I look them in the eye and ask them, "Do you want to be rich, or do you just want a job? If you want to be rich, get ready for the wildest ride of your life. I'm not trying to make friends with you. I don't get emotionally involved. Are you in or are you out?"

Over time, those I employ have come to respect that in me. They've looked at my past successes, and they've talked to my employees and ex-partners, all of whom would say, "Yeah, maybe he is an asshole, or a slave driver, or whatever. But he's made me a *lot* of money." And those people have become a vital part of every team I've assembled.

Speaking of which, you may be wondering whatever happened to John Freeman, the software genius behind the creation of a fantastic and innovative product. He never quit his job at Suncor. He worked there 9 to 5, sometimes coming to my house at night to rewrite the software to fit as many printers and plotters as possible. Years later, John left SoftKey, but he held on to some stock. And since we would eventually become a multimillion-dollar global empire employing more than three thousand people, he did very, very well perfecting that one great idea.

YOU DON'T BUILD WEALTH PART TIME

If you're going to start a business, if you're going to hire people, then they will be relying on their jobs to feed their families. That's a big deal. Forget 9 to 5. You have to work all day, every day, and often harder than everyone else, to ensure that. I tell people that if they weren't here on Saturday, don't bother coming in on Sunday. (Or the following Monday, for that matter. Remember: "Next!")

I get up at four-thirty in the morning and I go to bed sometimes as late as midnight. Those early-morning hours are very important: it's quiet, so I can get stuff done uninterrupted. I've got the time to do what I have to do before the day starts. I expect everyone who works for me to keep the same odd and ridiculous hours. I want to be able to call my operations manager at any time, day or night, and have sales numbers at the ready. I don't care if his wife's trying to sleep next to him, or if his girlfriend's one night a week with him is now ruined. I'm not making friends. I'm making money. A lot of relationships don't survive in the kind of environment that requires that level of commitment. When teams go through incredible stress, change, and growth together, it can be very bonding. Your work relationships begin to feel more familial, and your familial relationships take more work. Coming home to a quiet house after a long day doing million- and sometimes billion-dollar deals can almost feel anticlimatic. I try hard to leave work at work, and to be *home* when I am home, but I don't always pull it off. Still, I am not someone who apologizes for bringing my BlackBerry to the dinner table or to bed. What can I say? Building a company is all-consuming and addictive. I'm the first to admit it. Luckily, I've always teamed up with people who suffer from the same affliction.

THE ANATOMY OF
THE PERFECT TEAM

As you begin to form your team (which includes your life partner or spouse), accept that it must evolve as your company grows and changes. Stay fluid and flexible in this phase, and be merciless about who gets to remain in the boat. Anyone not contributing to the growth of the company gets thrown overboard. Does your business have the people it needs to be the strongest, most competitive team in the field? If you're missing any of these important players, or if you've got them and they're underperforming, your business is going to suffer the consequences.

1. **The Business Partner.** I have only ever made money working in a partnership, and I've been blessed by every single partner I've had. You may wonder how an egomaniac like me can thrive in a partnership. As I've said before, I know my weaknesses, so I've always known that mine cannot be the only voice of the company. My voice must be joined by that of someone with a different take and a new perspective on our growing enterprise. In chapter 6, I hone in on how to help your partnerships thrive, but for me, a partnership is a money-making dynamic.

2. **The Numbers Expert.** This person is often your chief financial officer, the third leg of the sturdy stool. Your numbers expert is someone who knows every inch of the company, who gets up a few minutes earlier than you and goes to bed a little later. They're you, but a swifter version, because they're not

carrying the weight of the company on their shoulders, though they could run the place if they had to. If you called your CFO in the middle of the night for a bit of information, he or she could retrieve it without turning on the lights. That's because it's lodged in his or her brain.

3. **The Sober Second Thinker.** Sometimes this is your legal arm, or your head of publicity, and this individual is just about the only person who can say no to you and to whom you'll listen without question. Because his or her no is protecting you legally, financially, or publicly.

4. **The Efficiency Expert.** This person's not my assistant. At O'Leary Funds, Anita Bell is my executive in charge of syndication, and she makes a pantload of cash. Because she needs to know where I am at all times and where to put me to sell my funds, it's more efficient for her to be in charge of protecting my time rather than just managing it, which my assistant does. My efficiency expert has the company's info at her fingertips, and she keeps a keen eye on human resources.

5. **The Hometeam Leader.** The most important partner I had was my wife, Linda, who, like my work partner, possessed all the skills and traits I lacked. She was kind and patient where I was a jerk, serious when I could be a joker, firm when I was a pushover with the kids (since I tended to parent with guilt because I wasn't around a lot). Without her, I would have never achieved the things I have. She kept the home fires burning while I dug the coal to keep them lit.

CHAPTER FIVE

HOW SMALL COMPANIES CAN BECOME GIANTS

DON'T COMPETE WHEN YOU CAN COMBINE

The more ubiquitous SoftKey became in the '80s, the more our competitors came to us asking to be included under our brand umbrella. By the early '90s, a dramatic shift had occurred in the industry when the price of personal computers plummeted. As they became more affordable, the software industry was pressured to drop its prices, too. Families were beginning to use their computers not just for home offices but for educational and entertainment purposes.

As a marketer, I paid particular attention to educational software and the reasons why consumers were buying it. I knew from experience as a parent and as a kid with a learning disability that parents always want their children to have educational advantages. And they'll go to any length to get them. I thought of my mother, who did everything in her power to get me the reading and writing help I needed—the after-school tutors, the special books, finding Margie Golick, bringing me to Montreal Children's Hospital every day for weeks and months. If an expensive computer and pricey software had promised a solution, my mother would have been the first in line at Best Buy. What motivated her was no different from what drove mothers in the digital age— except that mothers in the '90s had new computerized tools and newfangled games to help teach their kids, and I wanted SoftKey to be at the vanguard of those products.

But our company was struggling. Logistics were a problem. We had expanded our software line so quickly, I couldn't get our product out the door fast enough, couldn't fill orders, couldn't get the product from A to B in a timely fashion. This was the job of the operations department, and operations have never been my strength.

A guy named Michael Perik was watching our bottom line go from black to red from the confines of a private equity firm that had put almost a million dollars into SoftKey. He called me one day to chat, to suss out what was going wrong at SoftKey, because he was tasked with keeping an eye on his firm's investment. We were losing money, and his bosses weren't happy. We met to talk about what could be done about that, and Mike spotted several holes in our logistics and operations departments. The flow of goods was clogged in key spots related to distribution and sales. Again, these are my blind spots, but anyone could see that if those departments weren't overhauled and the problems remedied, we were sunk.

Rather than implement any suggestions Perik had made, I gave him an offer he couldn't refuse: I asked him to leave his firm

Michael Perik and me in the early days of SoftKey.

and join SoftKey, in exchange for an equal partnership; he'd take over finance and operations, leaving me sales and marketing. I'd become the president; he'd be the CEO. I barely knew the guy, but I could tell right away that he was exactly what my company needed. His assessment of the problems and his solutions made total sense to me. I knew that I wanted him on board. He was the salt to my pepper, quiet and cerebral where I was bombastic and visceral. My gut said this was the kind of guy who could ground me.

The only way to convince Perik to walk away from his lucrative profession was to make him a lucrative offer. That's why I get hot-headed with entrepreneurs on *Dragons' Den* who balk at handing over hefty percentages of their company to me. If you want my investment and my expertise, it comes at a price. I never hesitated to give Perik an equal partnership because I knew that without his ability to straighten out those divisions, without his expertise in dealing with legal and accounting, without his tempering force, I would have owned 100 percent of a dead company.

EVERY EMPLOYEE IS A COST

Perik said yes to my offer, and together we did something no tech company had ever done before: we began to aggressively apply the principles of consumer-goods marketing to the software industry. Chief among these principles was cutting costs. I also changed the way I managed our clients. Prior to Perik coming aboard, I thought it was good enough to mail out a quarterly prospectus. But shareholders have to know you, see you, feel the firmness of your handshake, he said. So I began flying all over the world, attending conferences, meeting manufacturers and local managers. We were a powerful partnership. Perik was able to streamline vital wings of the company, so that when I thought of a new product, we could get it on the market quickly. The Key brand was unlimited, after all. In the mid-'90s, we launched KeyDesign Center 3-D for architects and designers to create three-dimensional renderings of living and work spaces. It had one hundred pre-built scenes and almost a thousand different ways to furnish the rooms. Every quarter, we released new Key titles, including KeyCAD, KeyFont, and KeyOrgChart.

We also convinced Scott Murray, our audit manager from an outside accounting firm, to come aboard. Murray was a genius with numbers, and we needed that kind of exacting focus on our bottom line. He became an integral part of our team, with his superhuman ability to locate and eliminate bloat.

We were that solid three-legged stool, Perik, Murray, and me. We began to put our expertise to work, looking at every employee we hired as a cost. Every chair was occupied by someone who took money away from our shareholders and our bottom line. If they weren't performing, they were whacked. We also had to massively expand our distribution chains. If software was a consumer good, it needed to be placed in as many consumer hands as possible. We could no longer just sell at specialty shops and computer accessory stores. We had to establish distribution chains that fed SoftKey into big-box stores, bookstores, video stores, music stores, and even, to the astonishment of our competitors, grocery stores. We began to look around at our competition, with an eye not toward beating them but rather eating them up. We realized that instead of out-selling our competitors, it would make our lives easier if we knew what products were coming down the pipelines, and the only way to know that was to own them. And frankly, they couldn't sue us if we were shareholders. We had a powerful team. I had command of the sales and marketing wing, Perik was the strategist and opera-tions guru, and Murray was the numbers guy with an eagle eye on costs. We rounded out our key team when I recruited Tony Bordon, who was working for one of our distributors out of New York. At first, he turned me down. Then he stopped taking my calls. So I

My partnership with Scott Murray (left) and Michael Perik (middle) lasted over a decade. At our zenith, we were the most feared management team in the consumer software industry as we gobbled up competitors and drove down software prices. I loved it!

had no choice but to get his home number and call him one Saturday morning, making him a final lucrative offer while he was still wiping the sleep out of his eyes. He finally relented.

"You're a tireless bastard, O'Leary."

"Welcome aboard. You start tomorrow."

"But it's Sunday."

"I know."

SPEND TO GROW, BUT ONLY ON VITALS

With our team intact, SoftKey went on an industry-wide acquisitions binge. At first, we focused on office productivity software because that's what the Key brands were known for: maps, calendars, dictionaries, fonts, and word processing. So we courted companies such as WordStar out of Novato, California, which published, among other titles, the *American Heritage Dictionary*. That acquisition included one of WordStar's best salesmen, a guy named David Patrick, who quickly rose through SoftKey's ranks. We got lucky that way with a number of mergers. We snagged some great companies that often came with great people.

During this phase of our growth, Perik, Murray, and I would often stay at cheap hotels, eating breakfast on a picnic table out back, maybe hitting a Burger King drive-thru for dinner. Money was tight. Until we had more cash flow, we did not spend a dime on anything that didn't have to do with making money and growing the business. At the same time, we were in talks with another industry giant, Spinnaker Software, out of Boston. Spinnaker had an impressive list of reference products, including WindowWorks, a precursor to Microsoft's Windows, which would launch a few years later. Instead of choosing between the two, we made a bid for both Spinnaker and WordStar. SoftKey, the little company that started in my basement on Shaw Street in Toronto, became the first company ever to complete a three-way cross-border international merger. Boston became our new headquarters, and in 1993, I moved Linda and our baby daughter, Savannah, down to the States, where a year later we had our son, Trevor. We were now called SoftKey International and were trading on the NASDAQ, with $120 million in revenues on our books. But we weren't done yet.

THE BUYER SETS THE PRICE

In the early '90s, soon after Walmart began to sell affordable home computers, the retailer made an industry-wide announcement that it was allocating a significant chunk of its shelf space to consumer software. I clamored for a pitch meeting. Consider this: according to the U.S. Census Bureau, in 1984, when I first started in the software business, less than 10 percent of American homes had a computer. By 1997, that figued had jumped to 36 percent. Today that percentage has more than doubled.

The home computer trend had caught fire and spread to Walmart's clientele. Computers weren't just for rich people anymore, and neither was software. And since everyone shopped at Walmart, I figured everyone needed SoftKey. I made it clear to Walmart that our company was the only one that covered all of a consumer's needs, from education to entertainment. I got the meeting and flew down to Arkansas.

"And we're the cheapest," I concluded. "Our prices average about $39.95 per package."

The Walmart buyer didn't blink. He just sat back in his chair, cradling the back of his head in his hands. He had a thick

Southern accent, suspenders, and a cigar. (You could still smoke in your office back then.)

"How much did y'all say you want to sell your software for?"

"About forty bucks a package."

Long, slow whistle.

"See, we don't sell stuff that expensive. Here, y'all are gonna sell your computer stuff for about $19.99."

I nearly spat out my Tab. At that price, in order to make a profit, we'd have to sell to Walmart for $12.49! I looked up at the massive camera over his head, and then back at the one behind me recording our conversation. Walmart taped all their meetings, but for a second I thought maybe I was on *Candid Camera*.

"Er. That's not possible," I said, half-laughing. "Do you have any idea what goes into developing and making software?"

"Nope," he said, "and I don't care. Y'all want my four linear feet of shelf space, then you gotta sell whatever it is you're selling for $19.99. Last year, I sold fishing boots there. Last month, towels. For now, I'm told it's gonna be software. After that, who knows? Meanwhile, I don't care whose software I sell. All I know is it's not gonna cost $39.95, 'cause nothing sells at that price, no matter how fancy. Not here, anyway."

I was quiet. Our prices were already among the lowest in the industry. The buyer looked up at me as if he was astonished I'd been sitting there all along.

"Well, son, if you can't figure out how to sell your software for $19.99, I got six guys in the waiting room who can."

I wanted that order. I wanted that shelf space. I told him it wouldn't be a problem.

"That's the right answer," he said, shaking my hand.

I took out my ten-pound brick of a cell phone, whipped up the two-foot-long antenna, and called Perik back in Toronto.

"I got good news and I got bad news. Good news is I got a $5-million purchase order from Walmart. Bad news is we have to retail our products for half the price we sell to everyone else."

Another long, slow whistle.

"How are we going to produce this?" I asked. It was my turn for some good news.

"That's not a production problem," he said, adding to the bad news. "It's a marketing problem. You're the marketer. Solve it."

LIVER IS TO READING WHAT FISH IS TO MATH

It wasn't unusual in those days to spend $100 on a piece of basic accounting software, something that would help you balance the books for your small business or do your taxes. Margins were good at those price points, but volume wasn't. The market for expensive consumer software was shrinking right along with the price of computers. We had to cut costs.

I took a long look at the research-and-development team that worked on producing new programs for SoftKey. That team was the beginning of a very expensive assembly line. After code was written, products had to be tested, boxes designed, and CDs stamped, packaged, shipped, and marketed. Every time we launched a new program, we had to spend a small fortune. Think about the variety of products we offered back then: tax software, reference materials like dictionaries and encyclopedias, complicated 3-D design programs. Each was different in its own way, and each required a completely different set of skills to create and produce. And that's just to manufacture the software. Selling different kinds of software to different markets was also expensive. In fact, SoftKey's research-and-development team accounted for a whopping 24 percent of our operating budget; advertising and promoting our new titles sucked up another 12 percent. How were we supposed to get an edge over our competition when we were bleeding money just by making new products?

When I returned from Arkansas, I called an emergency meeting. Picture a big, bright room with a long oval table made of blond wood, a dozen black chairs surrounding it, each occupied by a member of an elite team of software executives: Michael Perik, my partner; Scott Murray, our CFO; David Patrick, now head of SoftKey worldwide sales; and Tony Bordon, head of the all-important U.S. market. Moments later, we were joined by Jack Dolan, our head of licensing and OEM sales, and Sanjay Khosla, who worked on production and logistics and made those tiny crucial adjustments that would save us a fortune. He once shaved one-sixteenth of a cent off costs by changing the ink on a package from red to pink. Another time, for packages shipped abroad, he switched to a cardboard stock that was a fraction of a centimeter thinner. When you sell in the tens of millions, these changes mean money in the bank. You could say he was the arms expert in SoftKey's war on the competition.

I looked around the table that day and thought, "This is like the Hall of Justice, except we are the superheroes of capitalism." Maybe some people wouldn't get off on that, but I certainly did.

I laid out our mandate. "We have to come up with a new line of software that Walmart can retail for about twenty bucks, which means to make a profit we have to sell it to Walmart for about twelve bucks."

Here's what I love most about that team: this was not a problem to them—this was a challenge. And here's what I still believe: these are the kinds of challenges that salespeople tackle better than managers or engineers. Salespeople understand the most important trigger in the whole chain—what makes people buy. No matter how great the product, if consumers aren't picking it up, the business will die. That's why I believe salespeople are the most important cog in the benevolent machinery of capitalism.

We began by tossing around a few in-store scenarios. Sanjay came up with the brilliant idea of losing the boxes and manuals altogether. We'd package our Walmart line of software in shiny jewel cases, with instructions printed in booklets. And we'd build special racks to house them.

"We should insist that Walmart place the racks by the checkout," Sanjay said, "so buying software will start to feel like a last-minute purchase—like picking up a magazine or a paperback."

We didn't know it at the time, but that would go on to become a revolutionary idea, the moment that software lost its last remaining patina of "specialty product."

The next decision we made was to narrow Walmart's product line to just the big sellers: anything to do with educational software—particularly reading and math programs.

"They're our most popular products," David Patrick pointed out. "So let's just give them that to start with. Keeps it focused and simple."

"Besides, the educational stuff will be less expensive to produce en masse," said Tony Bordon, barely looking up from his notes. "The software engines themselves don't change much from lesson to lesson, right? Mostly just the graphics."

"That's true," I said.

And that is when it struck me—a game-changing idea. *Reading and math are to software marketing what liver and fish are to the cat food industry.*

"Comrades, we are about to crack this industry wide open," I said. I explained how two flavors were the bases upon which Nabisco built a multimillion-dollar cat food empire. Just as Nabisco streamlined production by building multiple flavors atop two cat food bases, we would build new scenarios and challenges on top of the two basic engines that underpinned our educational products: reading and math. And just like that, I reinvigorated the most important lesson I'd learned at my stint with Nabisco and applied it to my software company. After all, what's the difference between the consumer needs of a three-year-old child and those of a cat? Not much. The parent buys for the kid *and* the cat.

"And let me tell you," I added, "Walmart's right. Those same parents who'd rather pay pennies for a tin of cat food want to spend only twenty bucks for software."

"Well, if we're going to create a new product line," said Scott Murray, "we should come up with a new name."

Seconds later, and from the deepest, darkest corners of my marketer's brain, I piped up and said, "Titanium Seal!"

I was experiencing that rare and marvelous feeling of being on the same wavelength as my colleagues *and* being supernaturally connected to an invisible wire feeding inspiration to my brain.

"Titanium Seal. I like it," said Michael. "But what does it mean?"

"Doesn't matter. It sounds exclusive. And expensive," I said. "Plus, it'll differentiate the SoftKey products we sell to Walmart from the ones we sell elsewhere."

It was a history-making meeting.

VOLUME TRUMPS PRICE

The combined forces of our emergency-meeting superpowers worked. Walmart couldn't stock the new racks fast enough. And our price plunge changed not only our company but also the entire industry. Within the year, we had applied those revolutionary cost-cutting ideas to all of our products, and then we went after some other popular ones as well. The number-one design software at the time was Corel Draw, which sold for more than $400 a package. Rather than invent a cheaper version of Corel Draw from scratch, I approached Corel and asked them to license a more basic version of their professional design software. They told me to go away. I persisted. I told them I could sell more in a week than they sold in a year. Finally, Corel relented, licensing a cheaper version of Corel Draw that we rebranded and sold for $9.99. It went through the roof, selling millions of units. It was a great deal for them, because I was getting into distribution channels they didn't have access to, like Zellers and Walmart. Back then, when you wrote an innovative piece of software, it was often plagiarized, duplicated, and ripped off. As far as Corel was concerned, it was better to duplicate the program with my company's help, and at least make some money out of it, rather than to let consumers find a way to get the product for free.

Adobe also put out pricey font software, selling it for $99.99. I found a designer in Chicago willing to create similar fonts—hundreds of them—altering each almost imperceptibly, rendering them different enough that we weren't breaking copyright laws. Then we sold the software for $9.99. It was a huge hit—we sold millions of copies. Everyone and their mother tried to sue us for that. No one was successful. If a company had innovative software that was selling big, I put out a version of it, right on its heels. They carved the path, and I followed, like a seagull trailing a bloated cruise ship. One company would put out expensive dictionary software; we put out KeyDictionary. Someone else put together elaborate map software; we'd put out KeyMaps, always at that attractive price point: $9.99. We could barely keep up with demand. We fired two-thirds of our development team, and our costs in that department dropped from 24 percent to 11 percent, giving us a devastating edge over our competition. Our stock price rose, we raised capital, and we went on an aggressive and unprecedented buying spree, acquiring several of our most vicious competitors. Why compete against them when you can own them?

Once these smaller companies were under our wing, we'd absorb their bestsellers under the Key brand of SoftKey, then sell them for a lot less. Even before one line of code was written, we had to ask one fundamental question: Is this product worth spending $100,000 to produce? Most of the time, the answer was no. We no longer allowed software developers to set the price point on our products. That was none of their business, and certainly not their area of expertise. Our brand, SoftKey, and our distribution channels were proprietary, and not to be messed with. Code writers were a dime a dozen. I told them the price, and they built the software accordingly. If they didn't like it, they moved on to another company, and since we were on a buying spree, it wasn't uncommon for people I fired to pop up again in a company I'd just bought. It was like a game of Whack-a-Programmer.

I had very vocal critics, people who called me a schlockmeister, accusing me of treating software like Fig Newtons. And to them, I said, "You are right. And why shouldn't I?" My belief was this: educational software shouldn't be available only to the children of the affluent. Anyone should be able to buy products that entertain or educate them. Our target market was anyone with a computer and a desire to expand their knowledge or skill set. SoftKey revolutionized the industry by opening up massive retail channels that eventually included Sears, Montgomery Ward, Home Depot, Sam's Club, Costco, and OfficeMax, along with Zellers and Walmart.

Before us, no software company had ever put so much emphasis on management, product testing, package design, and control of the distribution chain. We had to. By then, specialty-store chains that focused only on selling software had completely collapsed. We were smart to have established our product in big-box stores and retail giants, because we weren't scrambling when the small computer-store chains disappeared. Smarter still, we remained flexible on our pricing, because we realized our empire would die if our products remained on the shelf. If our products weren't moving, none of our other efforts mattered. I might have been the most hated man in the industry, but SoftKey was a lucrative and growing company, with unprecedented sales figures. And because of the incredible strength of our partnership, we were about to get much, much bigger.

FIVE RULES FOR SUCCESSFUL PARTNERSHIPS

There are tons of books on how to have a happy marriage. But keeping your business partnership healthy is an equally important goal, because it's a direct reflection of the health of the company. Here are a few pointers on how to keep your partnerships vital and strong:

1. **Find someone whose strengths are *precisely* your weaknesses. Have very little overlap.** Michael Perik was my CEO. He was in charge of our operations. Without him, our company would have been dead in the water. Scott Murray was the CFO. He was in charge of our finances. Without him, we would never have been able to acquire the companies we acquired, and we would never have eventually sold our company, The Learning Company (TLC), for billions. I was in charge of sales and marketing, and of getting our product in front of as many consumers as possible. Among the three of us, there were simply no gaps in the armor. We rarely made mistakes. Sales, marketing, finance, operations—we had it covered. As a team, we were brilliant and envied, and at our peak, I would go so far as to say we were loathed. But we buoyed each other, and we thrived in that environment.

2. **Leave your ego at the door.** Too many endeavors fail because one partner won't give up the reins to another. Egos are the biggest culprits. I never suffered from that. In fact, my partners

and I have made developing "bench strength" a priority. It's a baseball term that means that although you have your strongest players in the field, you cultivate a hell of a tight backup team on the bench, ready to jump in and save the day if your starters can't. Companies that don't do that don't survive. And they often don't do that because they think their hotshot CEOs, CFOs, and presidents are irreplaceable. They are not. Everyone is replaceable, even you. Never forget that.

3. **Establish a common goal.** I didn't interfere with the line of command. I didn't question the decisions of my top-tier team players because we had already established our common goal and never veered from it: to conquer the market at all costs. I knew they'd do whatever it took to achieve that goal, and they accorded me the same leeway with sales and marketing, the divisions I helmed.

4. **Never undermine your partners in public, even when you think they're wrong.** Disagreements and divisions must be dealt with in private. Never let your shareholders or employees see you disagree. Communicate until you're back on the same page again with a viable solution. It's a lot like good parenting. Once a kid sees a crack in the united parental front, it's over. Disagree in private, but your public partnership must be impenetrable.

5. **It's always about the company.** Every move, every decision, every disagreement must be about the company. It's never personal. Partner with people who get that; otherwise, they'll

be working out their latent family issues all over your bottom line. The people you partner with are not your husband, your wife, or your brother or sister. They're your business partners. It may feel like you're closer to them than you are to your own spouse, but at the end of the day it's always, always, *always* about the money.

CHAPTER SIX

BE FIRST, FAST, AND FEROCIOUS

FOCUS ON THE BEST, DUMP THE REST

Flush with cash, SoftKey made a vital decision. We needed to focus on a specialty, and since we had discovered a winning formula in developing products out of basic reading and math engines, we decided to move away from selling dictionaries and encyclopedias—which people bought only once—and turn our attention toward educational software that people turned to again and again. That meant it was time to go after the great white shark of the educational software industry: The Learning Company. TLC had the massively popular Reader Rabbit series. Reader Rabbit was a remarkably smart gray bunny—often dressed in a red T-shirt—that taught kids from preschool through grade two how to read. Problem was, in August 1995, TLC announced plans to merge with Brøderbund, a California company that distributed the

Reader Rabbit Learning Company Software.

video games Myst and Riven, as well as the beautifully produced Carmen Sandiego series, which taught kids about geography. They were all huge sellers. The press release announcing the potential merger was studded with words like *delighted, looking forward to,* and *excellent strategic match,* as if it had been ripped from the pages of *The New York Times*'s Vows section.

Suddenly, acquiring TLC wasn't an option; it was a mandate. So like any ardent suitor, we did what we had to do to make it impossible for TLC to say no. Perik, Murray, and I realized that in order to pull off a bigger offer than Brøderbund's, we would have to do a lot of work to make SoftKey the more attractive partner. We had to get a little bigger. The deadline to top Brøderbund's offer was tight, so over a ten-day period during the summer of 1995, we acquired the Minnesota Educational Computing

Corporation for about $450 million in stock. MECC had the Oregon Trail, software about the American pioneering days. MECC had also established the golden goose of distribution channels—public schools in Florida, California, Texas, and New York. By Thanksgiving of that year, we'd met up with the Chicago publishing powerhouse Tribune Company and brought them on as shareholders. Then we bought their software wing, Compton's. That gave us further credibility in the educational space. It was as though we were saying to TLC, "Look what we've got!"

With these companies headquartered from California to Illinois, I must have flown across the country every other day. We were merging and acquiring at such an incredible rate that in order to speed up company integrations, we'd tell our employees in Boston handling the mergers that they couldn't go home until the integration process was complete. You'd be amazed at how fast the process went.

PEOPLE AREN'T AS COMPETITIVE
AS THEY ARE GREEDY

Flush from our recent acquisitions, and with the backing of our esteemed private-equity firms, Thomas H. Lee and Bain Capital, we put together $600 million in cash and made our hostile bid for TLC. Shock waves rippled through the industry. What balls! A company no one had heard of a few months ago was now throwing down $600 million in cash, a sum we knew TLC shareholders would have been ridiculously stupid to turn down. And here's another thing I've learned: if you want to buy a company, don't talk to the president or CEO. He or she is often just an employee. Go straight to the shareholders and dangle big bucks in front of their faces. I can't tell you how many times a sneering executive or a pompous president told me that he would never let SoftKey in the door, that SoftKey wasn't "good enough" to own his precious company. It never fails to amuse me, the idea that those CEOs and presidents, with their fancy cars and their private elevators, forgot that they were indeed just employees. They forgot that they served the shareholders, and as long as the shareholders were happy with their performance, they'd get to keep their jobs. But they failed to consider that their shareholders—for the right price—would be all too happy to hand over a company, and if those CEOs and presidents didn't own stock, they'd get whacked. That's what I love about money: its motives are predictable, and its only allegiance is to itself.

People are greedy. I learned that in Psychology 101. People are also competitive. But had I known it when I was in school, I would have told my psych professors that when it comes to money, people are infinitely greedier than they are competitive. Everyone folds for the right price. For TLC, that right price was $600 million. Why? Because it was $100 million more than Brøderbund's offer.

TLC accepted our offer, and it was a bit of a shotgun wedding— no gushy Style section announcement, but it did make the front page of all the main financial papers across the country. By the way, two years later we bought Brøderbund for a fraction of what they'd been worth when they made their play for TLC—and a weak play it was. The lesson here is that Brøderbund should have been ferocious when they had the chance. And if our critics were right and we overpaid for TLC by $100 million, we made it back, and then some, when we acquired Brøderbund at such a deep discount.

With TLC, we'd now have access to all the *Sesame Street* characters, the *Schoolhouse Rock* cartoons, the wildly popular Baby-sitters Club, and the classic Madeline character. We'd also have agreements with *Sports Illustrated,* and had plans to put out a CD-ROM Swimsuit Calendar. And of course, we owned the entire Reader Rabbit line, which included Mat the Mouse and Sam the Lion—endless recipes for our math and reading software engines.

Scott Murray suggested that since we were going to move off the NASDAQ and start trading on the New York Stock Exchange, it would be easier for SoftKey to just adopt The Learning Company's name and trading symbol. The day we finally hit the NYSE was a red-letter day for me. We were invited to ring the bell at the day's opening. I hired a guy to dress up as Reader Rabbit and accompany us onto the trading floor. It was one hell of a photo op.

Listing The Learning Company on the New York Stock Exchange. From left to right: Lamar Alexander, then a director and now a U.S. senator; NYSE official; Reader Rabbit; Mike Perik; and me.

With our transformation into an educational software giant complete, we took a well-needed break over the holidays, which meant our meetings moved to the beaches of St. Bart's from downtown Boston. Word soon reached us that the president and CEO of The Learning Company had resigned to protest our hostile takeover. Babies, I thought. Good. Let them go. But Perik and I realized that this was one integration we would have to handle personally. After the holidays, we slapped on suits and ties and flew to California, fully expecting to find TLC's suite of offices empty, a few stray CD boxes piled in a corner, crumpled Kleenex from all the bawling, phone cords dangling, the halls echoing with petulance.

But we were mistaken. There were a lot of employees left—some defiant, some enthusiastic, all wondering about the next steps. We loosened our ties and introduced ourselves. Looking around the room, the first thing I realized was no one wore ties out there. Second thing I realized was we would have to speak individually to each employee, from the head programmers to the secretaries, to communicate our plan for the future and to figure out exactly who to fire. Here's how a typical conversation would go: I'd meet with a brand manager, say, to explain that her boutique software company had to adapt to a new way of thinking. The days of $79.99 software were over, I'd tell her. We make software that is affordable and accessible, I'd explain. So what I need you to do is show me a product that we can sell for $19.99, one that isn't going to cannibalize product we already have on the shelf. Often, the brand manager would comply. But sometimes I'd hear something like this:

"Forget it. What you're doing is wrong. I don't want to taint my brand. You're watering down something we've spent years developing, which has a dedicated fan base that expects a certain level of polish."

My response: "You're fired. Who's the *assistant* brand manager?"

Moments later, the assistant brand manager would enter, trembling.

"What's your name?" I'd ask.

"Susan Blah-de-blah."

"Susan, tell me, do you have a product that we can sell for $19.99?"

"Um. Yeah, I do. I think. As a matter of fact . . ."

And that's how it went.

IF YOU WANT SOMETHING, ASK FOR IT

While shopping for T-shirts that first night in California, we realized we'd be there for at least three months to negotiate the handover. Later, over some fine Chablis at a much nicer hotel than the Holiday Inn, I pored over TLC's software catalog, labeling products either a "dog" or a "gem." Each product got either a big D scribbled on it or a G. All the word-processing software got a D because we were not going to compete with Microsoft. It was too expensive. Instead, we were going to completely own the market Microsoft had abandoned: education. Also, at that time (believe it or not), Apple Computer was a dying company. Their hardware was expensive, not widely available, and the Mac desktops looked like hair dryers. Schools were starting to replace them with slicker, cheaper PCs. We were spending too much money making software products for such a tiny sliver of the market. I called my new California assistant and told her to get me an appointment with Steve Jobs at Apple. She nearly choked on her organic smoothie. Despite warnings and pleas from Silicon Valley know-it-alls who considered Jobs the great oracle of the West Coast, she arranged the meeting. Jobs met with few people, but he knew TLC was the company that made Mac-compatible software for the rare public school outfitted with Mac desktops. So our company effectively made it possible for his products to even *be* in the public school system. The way I saw it, he had little choice but to give me half an hour. Without our Mac-compatible line of software, his desktops would be turned into coatracks, and he knew it.

I flew to Cupertino, California. Jobs was on time for our 9 a.m. meeting; trailing him were his assistant and two other silent-type guys. We shook hands and I got to the point. I told him it cost me $50 million to make my software Mac-compatible. I told him he was losing serious market share in the schools. If he wanted TLC to continue to provide Mac-compatible software, I said, he'd have to foot that bill. The remainder of our conversation went a little like this:

"How much do you want again?"

"Fifty million."

After an uncomfortable silence, Jobs said something along the lines of, "Are you kidding me, O'Leary?"

To which I replied, "No. I am not." I explained that he was losing market share, and that I was losing money helping him keep whatever market share he had. Even putting it that way didn't assuage him. He accused me of having unbelievable balls to fly up to Cupertino to ask for $50 million. I had hoped that he'd come around to my way of thinking. But no, Jobs stood up, stretched a little, and then told me to get the fuck out of his office. He seemed insistent that I not only leave, but also never, ever come back. He was one tough bastard.

In the parking lot, a little shaken but not very surprised, I whipped out my clamshell cell phone, found a hot spot near my rental car where I could get service, and called head office. Perik laughed when I got to the part about getting tossed to the curb.

"Oh, well," he said. "If you want $50 million, you have to ask for it, I guess."

My thinking was, at least I got to meet Steve Jobs. It was on his turf, sure, but it was a great way to announce that TLC was a major player in this market. The next quarter, we drastically reduced the number of products that were Mac-compatible, but we didn't cut them entirely. After all, there was always a chance this little company called Apple could turn things around, right?

VISION IS NOTHING WITHOUT A PLAN

I told you about the upside to a company's economic down cycle: when money is scarce, it heightens your senses. It attunes you to where you can slash to stay afloat. Tough times can be enlivening—exciting, almost. Well, TLC was in an up cycle, and we knew there could also be a downside to the massive growth we had experienced. Companies that get fat fast can also get sassy. Decisions can get mired in bureaucracy. Lines of command can get muddled. The period before streamlining can be the most dangerous time for a company, and we knew we were right in the middle of a treacherous zone. So to prevent any backward momentum, and to maintain the success we'd fought so hard to build, we knew we had to constantly and clearly communicate the company's goals and exactly how we were to achieve them. Vision is nothing if you don't have a plan to execute it. So we decided to pare everything down to just one key task: grow market share. Period. It was a task every manager in every far-flung corner of the new and expanded TLC could easily understand and then execute in their territory. I sent out missives explaining to our managers that when they woke up in the morning, I wanted them to pour boiling oil on our competitors—wipe them out, steal their market share, stop their growth, even if it meant litigating them into the Stone Age. At the end of the day, I wanted to know from these managers: Did we get more market share? Did we make more profit? Did we get that product listed in another retailer? Which employees lost their listings? How long will it take for them to clear out their desks? How fast can we replace them? I required my managers to email or phone me with details about how they had won more market share that day. I wanted to know if our competitors feared and hated us. And if they didn't, why not? That's how we got to be so successful. And I believe everyone who doesn't approach business this way will fail. Because here's the thing: in business, if you're not growing, you're dying.

My motives weren't evil. Quite the opposite. It was humbling to travel to the other side of the world, to stand in front of eager employees in, say, Germany, translator at my side, and realize that these people in this faraway city were supporting their families by working for my company. They had homes and mortgages, dreams and aspirations. I didn't know who they were, but they knew who I was. I was the face of TLC. That's when things started to change for me. I became even more ruthless about the competition because people were joining TLC by the hundreds, every month, in dozens of countries. That was enormous amount of responsibility, because livelihoods were at stake. I never took that for granted, never rested on my laurels.

Once, I went to meet our team in France after a big market correction had cut their stock in half. It was a critical blow because they had taken stock instead of cash in the sale of the company. When I entered the crowded boardroom, I could see a lot of panicked French faces waiting for me to tell them how bad I felt about the hit their stock had taken. That wasn't my approach.

"Look," I said, "I'm not here to apologize for the stock prices plummeting. Those prices will vary every day, and we've made a long-term investment in this company. We have no control over the ups and downs. So get over it. What I want to know is how we're going to make the next quarter in France. How are we going to grow market share and cripple our competition? That's all I'm here to talk about, because that's all we have any control over."

There was some French silence, followed by some French muttering. After the meeting, the employees shuffled out and got back to work.

Later, one of the managers admitted the company wasn't used to that kind of frank talk about money.

"Zey sink you're a heartless prick," he said, taking a sip from his white wine.

"I'm just a realist. Keep your eye off the stock and on growing market share, and it'll all turn out fine."

But here's the truth: I knew that if I panicked, they'd panic. If I didn't face the facts, how could they? If I obsessed about what couldn't be changed, so would they—and that could be deadly in an already volatile environment. In corporations, panic produces a kind of rigidity that kills the vital senses required to correct mistakes, regroup, and conquer. Never panic.

A few months later, that same manager called me and said that, over time, my pep talk had had a strangely reassuring effect on his staff. Turns out they cared about money, too—about their paychecks, their mortgages, and their investments with the company—so it didn't take long before that wing of the company was back in the black. Vive la France!

MONEY IS THE ONLY MOTIVATOR

I get a lot of pitches for those pajama-party corporate-bonding experiences—Outward Bound–type trips taken to hear some motivational bozo boost employees' morale. I'll tell you what motivates employees: money, plain and simple. I didn't travel to Germany and France to stand on a chair and hear myself talk. I went to outline a clear line of attack and to identify the key lieutenants who would head into battle with me. Their bravery and tenacity would be rewarded financially.

My money is my military, each dollar a soldier. I never send my money into battle unprepared and undefended. I send it out to conquer and to take currency prisoner and bring it back to me. The reason I instill this principle in my employees is that business is war—and we must grow every quarter. If they're successful in battle, they will get to see some of those glittering spoils. When I hear CEOs say people are motivated to succeed if you praise them, if you give them security or prestige, I say wrong, wrong, and wrong. The only thing that truly motivates people is money. And if that doesn't work, try *more* money.

ADAPT OR DIE

After the merger with TLC, we did find some terrific managers who really took to our way of doing business. Those who adapted thrived. Those who did not left. SoftKey had been known for not holding formal meetings. We popped in and out of each other's offices — often without knocking. We brought that style of communicating to TLC. There were no politics, no egos, but lots of healthy, vibrant debates, all in the name of making the company richer. The software industry was changing and growing at an alarming rate. Winning market share became thrilling and addictive. Some days were so frantic I would forget to eat, passing out at my desk from exhaustion, resenting the fact that I had to get any sleep at all.

With most of the key mergers and acquisitions complete, and all the fat trimmed, by the end of 1996 we could count almost three thousand people globally who were now working for TLC. Our products were sold in more than fifteen thousand retail outlets in forty-seven countries. We became the biggest educational software company in the world, twice the size of our closest competitor, with an enviable (and loyal) international distribution chain. We were lean, profitable, and growing. A year earlier, our annual sales had been $160 million. In 1996, they jumped to nearly $400 million. A year later, we would double that to $800 million. We won every major educational software award, and there wasn't a category, whether it was reading, math, or interactive, that we didn't dominate. And when we acquired Microsystems Software, we also owned Cyber Patrol, software that allowed parents to block inappropriate content on the Internet, a still-mysterious but rapidly growing commercial space. We knew the future of our company relied on conquering cyberspace, and we were beginning to get a foothold in that growing arena. I remember standing in front of shareholders in the early '90s, telling them that one day a personal computer would sell for less than $1,000.

"Not just every college student or every high school student," I said, "but every middle school student will have a personal computer, because they're all going to want to be on the Internet."

The shareholders looked at me as if I were from outer space. But this was our new mandate, and our new goal. Everyone employed by SoftKey had to get on that page or move on.

The Learning Company executives, the most feared management team in the consumer software market, in 1999. From top left to right: John Suske, Scott Murray, Greg Bestick, Bill Shupert, Neal Winneg, Allan Forsee, Tim Wright; middle row: Dave Patric, Tony Bordon, Ed Sattizhan, and me (lying on table). Mike Perik is missing from picture. (He might have taken it!)

HOW TO BE A
STAR EMPLOYEE

You already know what I do with problematic employees—I whack them, without exception. At least once on your path to entrepreneurship, you're going to have to work for someone. Here are a few things you can do right from the start that will help you avoid the ax and give you a firm foothold in the workplace. If you're in a position to hire, honing these attributes will also help you spot these same qualities in the winners who will come work for you.

1. **Pace yourself.** Chances are, you were hired because you're a hotshot, someone with that ineffable quality that gives you an advantage over your competitors. It's not time to relax— but instead of jumping right in, take some time to observe and assess. Get the lay of the land. Don't announce your hotshot-edness upon arrival. Rising stars already have a built-in trajectory. You don't need to accelerate the process.

2. **Take stock.** Not everyone becomes a partner, even if you're there at the inception of companies like Facebook or Google. But a lot of those early employees took stock rather than exorbitant wages. Today, they're stinking rich, the exceptions to the rule that you can't get wealthy working for other people. Taking stock shows faith in the company—plus, anything that ups the stakes ups the performance. It might mean a lower paycheck initially, but if you're passionate about the venture,

and feel your ideas will impact and influence the business, this is a good way to go. Remember, it's almost impossible to get rich without owning equity.

3. **Think beyond your borders.** If you really want to set yourself apart from your peers, beyond knowing everything there is to know about your company, douse yourself in details about your competitors. Read the trade papers, study the company taking away valuable clients, subscribe to their catalog, attend competitors' seminars, eat at the restaurants that leech your clientele. Don't be myopic. Learn from others' mistakes, and build on their innovations. If business is war, this is the espionage part.

4. **Don't brownnose the boss.** This should go without saying— but many employees think that buttering up the boss is the best way to rise above your colleagues. They think they're pulling off an undetectable, subtle manipulation. You're better off sidling up to the top salesperson, the star manager, the smart assistant, and gleaning from them the winning qualities that have made them a valuable part of a team. Which brings me to . . .

5. **Your desk says a lot about you.** Keep it clean and orderly, with some personal touches here and there: a photo, an award, reference materials. But avoid colorful, distracting detritus, mementos, stickers, and stuffed animals. In fact, if you work for me, and I see a stuffed animal in your workspace, I'll light it on fire. Then I'll fire you.

CHAPTER SEVEN

MAKING FORTUNES—
AND ENEMIES

IF ONE COMPANY COURTS YOU,
FLIRT WITH OTHERS

In 1997, I approached Pleasant Rowland, the creator and CEO of the increasingly popular American Girl doll brand. I wanted TLC to do for American Girl what we had been able to do with Reader Rabbit and the *Sesame Street* characters. Pleasant was fiercely protective of her brand, so getting the go-ahead to license just one of her gorgeously detailed historical dolls for just one of our products was a months-long process. TLC had built software called Opening Night, which allowed you to create a play that would star a character—in this case, the Molly McIntire doll. It was a layered, interactive game that was both engaging and visually stunning. After seeing how well it would showcase Molly and her story, Pleasant—finally, blessedly—said yes. I think she came to the reluctant conclusion that even the tactile and carefully crafted American Girl dolls needed to have some kind of digital presence.

It took us only a few weeks to write Molly into the software. The disc itself was packaged in a beautiful tin cookie box. Once it hit the shelves of Walmart, sales exploded. Opening Night was the biggest seller of the holiday season. People were scooping it up just for the collectible cookie tin.

We didn't know it at the time, but another company was keeping a close eye on all of this—Hasbro. The massive toy company's chief competitor was Mattel, which I knew was in the process of acquiring American Girl for $700 million. Hasbro saw what we could do for one doll in a doll empire, and they wanted our company to do that for them. Suddenly TLC had two built-in suitors—Hasbro and Mattel—both of whom needed to make a big, expensive technological leap into the largely unknown digital world. Instead of initiating talks with Hasbro, we got Mattel on the phone. This is what you do when you know one suitor wants you: you find out if there are any others so you can sell at the best price possible.

Jill Barad was a legend at Mattel, one of the few female CEOs helming a Fortune 500 company. She's the savvy marketing genius who took the Barbie brand from $250 million to $1.5 billion in annual sales, earning the moniker "The Woman Who Saved Barbie." So when she called and told Perik and me to come to the Waldorf-Astoria to meet Mattel and talk about a merger, we hopped on the next shuttle to New York, checking in the night before the meeting to prepare. We'd read about Barad, a woman who reportedly took a business call while undergoing an emergency cesarean section. She was our kind of partner.

The next day, the suite was packed with lawyers, bankers, and partners—mostly men—a corona of dark suits surrounding the only female, Jill Barad. It was a scene right out of *Jerry Maguire*, a popular movie at the time. Barad gazed at us from across the crowded hotel room, as if to say, "You, TLC, complete me." But unlike Tom Cruise with Renée Zellweger, Barad didn't have us at hello.

WEALTH HAPPENS WHEN YOU'RE NOT LOOKING

The old adage is "To properly split a log, don't aim for the top—aim for the block beneath it." Creating wealth is like chopping wood. Splitting the wood becomes something that just happens on the way down, as the ax meets the block. When you're building wealth, making money can't be the only aim. It can't be the bull's-eye. Becoming wealthy truly happens when you're pursuing the thing you love the most.

For me, my favorite pursuit is creating something other people want. I'm a marketer at heart. I love the art of figuring out what's needed, what's wanted, what'll sell. I love making the million tiny adjustments that polish this coveted thing into an object of perfection, and I love putting it in the hands of those who want it most. When it's perfect to its maker, perfect to its marketer, perfect to its distributor, perfect to its retailer, and perfect to the person who bought it, it's a great accomplishment and hugely satisfying to me as someone involved in its creation. So to become wealthy, you have to create something someone else wants to own. In the case of TLC, we created an entire company.

By 1998, we knew that TLC was about to undergo a massive overhaul. We would have to move our entire enterprise online, an incredibly expensive undertaking, but entirely unavoidable.

Everyone was doing business on the Internet, and increasingly, fewer and fewer people bought their software in retail outlets like Walmart. They went online and either found shareware or downloaded it illegally.

Mattel, the world's largest toy company, was facing a growth crisis at this time. Its flagship product, Barbie, was still a monolith on the market, but sales had begun to flag. Kids were dumping their dolls and cars and taking to their computers at alarming rates. Mattel wanted to capture their imaginations online, and they wanted to capture their parents' wallets offline.

Back in that posh suite at the Waldorf, Barad and her dark suits slid an offer across the table. It amounted to a stock swap—three quarters of a Mattel share for every TLC share. In 1998, their stock was trading at about $45 a share—not bad, but it had begun to drift down. Silently thrilled, we told them we'd take it under consideration, knowing we had to consult our own backers, Thomas H. Lee and Bain Capital.

The next day, in Boston, both of our firms said no. I nearly collapsed. I pleaded with them, reiterating that this was a huge exit, and that we needed the strength of Mattel's brands to launch TLC into the next century.

Thomas H. Lee himself was implacable. He said it wasn't enough. And as much as he loved the idea of the merger, Mattel, he said, wasn't in a position to undervalue TLC.

It was a bold decision to turn down Mattel's initial offer, but Lee was a major shareholder, and as Lee had pointed out, TLC's future was as bright as Mattel's was murky. Mattel probably needed us more than we needed them. I think Lee's strategy was to figure out how scared Barad was about the future of a Mattel without a TLC. And it worked. By balking at their original offer, Lee was able to squeeze 20 percent more out of Mattel. Barad came back with a counteroffer Lee couldn't refuse: 1.2 shares for every TLC share, valuing us at $4.2 billion, an astounding sum. I shook my head. What a brilliant strategy. Hell, what balls!

Perik and I looked at each other and said, "This is what it's all for. It's all come down to this." And we had Thomas H. Lee to thank for it.

We cracked open the champagne in celebration. But our celebration wasn't only because of the money. We were also celebrating the past decade of our lives, and toasting all the sacrifices we had made and the risks we had taken to arrive at this level. This was the apex of my career. I thought of that troubled student struggling to read, that scrappy kid who was told he wasn't good enough, that lonely teen in a far-flung military college. I remembered the times when SoftKey had come close to financial collapse, and how hard it had been for me to ask my mother for help. I thought of all the times that Linda packed up the kids and moved us, and how I was often on the road, leaving her to deal with the hard stuff. I had missed a lot as the kids grew up, no doubt about it. But embedded in those two words—*sacrifice* and *risk*—is the notion of payback, a time when it's all supposed to feel worth it. This was that time. And, yes, $4.2 billion made it all worthwhile.

It was a thrilling moment, but it was also humbling, then terrifying. For Mattel to get a reasonable return on their investment, we had to prove—and fast—that we had a foolproof plan to turn profit. It was time to show them that we could take their brands into the twenty-first century. But we knew the path ahead was strewn with challenges. Would Mattel, this age-old, venerable institution, be able to adapt to our vigorous way of doing business? Could we earn back those billions, and then some, combining their brands and our marketing savvy? How much would it cost to chart this new digital path? What would it take? Were we properly equipped?

We were confident. We felt prepared to prove what TLC could do. There were those who said Mattel overpaid for TLC, but let me tell you this: you couldn't find any naysayers among our shareholders.

NEVER ALIENATE YOUR MONEYMAKERS

The deal closed in record time. Barad faced little resistance from her shareholders, and because of Scott Murray's meticulous financial records, TLC breezed through due diligence. By May 1999, TLC was officially under Mattel's umbrella. It should have been a win-win situation, a merger made in heaven, one blessed with excellent timing, and a marriage between some of the most popular brands in the long history of toys and short history of virtual entertainment. After the acquisition, we joined Jill Barad and began to execute our plan for complete and total domination of the retail, interactive, and online toy and education markets around the world. We had a clear path, and access to an incredible storehouse of beloved brands. TLC was staffed with talented engineers and designers who were prepared to take Barbie, American Girl, Matchbox, and Hot Wheels, for starters, and make them interactive. We just needed the go-ahead from Barad and the various departments in charge of Mattel's brands.

Problems began to surface almost immediately. Mattel insisted on having its own CFO in place, which meant Scott Murray had to leave. He had been integral in helping TLC become a money-making monolith, but Mattel wanted its own internal hire in the post. The second big problem was the speed with which decisions were made. My first product was Learn to Type Barbie—a software program that taught girls proper finger placement and improved their typing speed. We had preorders from Walmart. We thought we could sell about a million units, and had already built the engine for our Mavis Beacon line of office software. The next step was to replace the Mavis character in the typing exercises with Barbie. We just needed the Barbie artwork. Simple. Done.

I put in the call, initiating the process to retrieve the Barbie graphic files. Some nameless Barbie brand manager called me back to explain that "releasing" Barbie material required Barbie paperwork and Barbie concept meetings, which every level of Barbie management needed to attend. All Barbie decisions—including the simple decision to allow us to retrieve Barbie graphics—would require management's Barbie sign-off.

But we had to ship the product in *six weeks*, I explained, a deadline TLC had never had a problem meeting.

The brand manager hung up on me.

I immediately dialed Jill Barad's assistant. Here's how a typical exchange would go:

"Hi. It's Kevin O'Leary. I need to talk to Jill."

"What's it about?"

"It doesn't matter what it's about. Put her on."

"Hold, please."

Sound of Muzak, my pen tapping.

"Mr. O'Leary, thank you for holding. I need to know the matter you wish to discuss with Ms. Barad."

"No, you don't. Put Ms. Barad on. I need to talk to her right now."

"Hold, please."

Muzak, pen tapping, top of my head beginning to simmer.

"Thank you for holding, Mr. O'Leary. Ms. Barad is in a meeting at the moment. She can phone you back between 3:15 and 3:25."

"No, she can't. No, she won't. I need to speak to her right fucking now."

"Hold, please."

"No. I can't hold. This can't wait. You let Jill know one of her largest shareholders would like her on the phone right now."

"Hold, please."

The top of my head would blow off. Then I'd hang up. And so it went.

CULTURE CLASHES CAN HOBBLE CORPORATIONS

Our conversations never really varied from that script. Barad's inner sanctum was impenetrable. When she did deign to take my call, I'd tell her that if we continued at this bureaucratic snail's pace, we would not get our product on the shelves in time to turn a profit. I'd tell her that if we continued to experience blockages to product development, we would not make those lofty quarterly projections that she had so confidently announced to shareholders. I'd explain that if she wasn't going to implement our infrastructure changes, we would piss off our retailers, a crime punishable by immediate termination at TLC. My pleas fell on deaf ears.

That's when I realized I was Employee Number 67008. Here's what I think of as one of the worst mistakes a CEO can make:

alienating the very people charged with helping the company grow. Apart from the obvious management differences we encountered post-merger, there was also a serious culture clash between TLC's and Mattel's working styles. TLC sold software in a fast-paced, ever-changing market, and our success relied on making difficult decisions swiftly to remain ahead of the next technological wave. Mattel manufactured toys—some beloved brands were forty years old, and they were sold through ancient retail distribution channels. The biggest stumbling block was integrating those two styles. After every merger or acquisition, the first order of business is always to identify and eliminate redundancies. But Mattel had the upper hand on those decisions because it was a bigger, older Fortune 500 company. I couldn't just whack underperformers and people biding their time until retirement—and believe me, there were a lot of office zombies sitting at desks as big as coffins. Every personnel change had to be put through that same painstaking decision factory. TLC employees were used to being viciously nimble, but that strength was not put to use in this new environment.

Looking back, I can identify two cancers that had taken root early and metastasized over the years Mattel had been in business: lack of urgency and arrogance. At TLC, we worked hard (and played hard). "Summer hours" at TLC meant that employees could maybe leave at noon on a Saturday. And if employees didn't come in on Saturday, they might as well clear their desks on Monday. We put in ten-, twelve-, even sixteen-hour days, and then hung out after work to decompress together. At Mattel, an eight-hour day was the norm, and you'd be hard pressed to find anyone at a desk at 3 p.m. on a Friday. This drove me insane.

If I hadn't been totally bald by then, I'd have ripped out my hair. My TLC staffers weren't used to working in a giant bureaucratic machine, and our key employees—many of whom had been with us for the better part of a decade—up and left. After our talented CFO was ousted, Mattel moved our finance and IT department from Cambridge to California, and in the move lost most of its records.

With operations vulnerable again, a dilemma that had almost sunk SoftKey before Perik came aboard, no one was keeping a critical eye on the flow of distribution. I was overwhelmed by sales and marketing and trying to launch Mattel's online component, so we barely noticed that software sales had begun to drop, then plummet. Problem was that retailing toys and retailing software are two very different enterprises. Software is cheap to make, stamped locally, so we always sent more stock than we knew would be sold so that shelves looked stuffed and bins overflowed. That meant unsold product was returned to us—no big deal. But those returns freaked out Mattel, because they were used to unsold merchandise being the store's problem. After all, most of their toys were manufactured overseas in China, so stores had to buy Mattel inventory outright. If anything didn't sell, the stores sucked up the loss, not Mattel. Mattel's executives thought that you fixed the so-called software returns problem by dropping TLC's established distribution channels and moving the software through Mattel's. That alienated our retailers even more because they didn't want to suddenly have to buy massive amounts of software outright to stuff the shelves. They didn't do that with toys; why should they do that with software? Then TLC's old distributors retaliated by blocking TLC's software, which was now

Mattel's software, from reaching consumers during a crucial back-to-school period. By the end of 1999, Mattel was hit with millions of dollars in international returns.

I also knew we would soon have to move any new software products and games to the Internet, and I knew it had to happen fast—as fast as we had shifted from the floppy disk to the CD-ROM five years earlier. But, again, nothing moved fast at Mattel. And by the late '90s, many tech start-ups were already starting to crack and lean. We knew our days were numbered. We knew we were fighting a losing battle. We thought we'd be part of a team that would steer a venerable company into the next century, but we were wrong. Perik and I were employees, a couple of corporate cogs to be ignored. I should have known from my days at Nabisco that I wasn't a corporate guy, and here I was, trying to make my square peg fit into the round hole of Mattel. I'd made a big mistake.

An anticipated profit of about $50 million in the third quarter of 1999 turned into a loss of $105 million. By the fourth quarter, that loss had ballooned to $184 million. The acquisition of The Learning Company by Mattel was seen as a disaster for Jill Barad. In light of these losses, she resigned.

Integrations have to be well planned. In my opinion, what Mattel should have sped up, they slowed down (product development). What they should have slowed down, they sped up (integration). What they should have kept the same, they changed (finance and operations). But there were other forces at work besides internal management issues. The overall toy market was about to go into a freefall, primarily because there were simply fewer kids under age fourteen to market to. The North American birth rate had been in decline for more than a decade. And children's play habits were changing faster than could have been predicted. These kids wanted their interactive video games, web-based toys, and newfangled gadgets—and they wanted them now. And once parents bought a gaming console and placed it in front of the family TV, every toy company lost market share, including Mattel.

The natural solution was to develop markets overseas, in places where the birth rates were actually on the rise. But price points for Barbie, American Girl, Hot Wheels, and other popular Mattel products were too high to close that market gap.

What worked for Mattel in the '50s and '60s was killing the company in the late '90s. Michael Perik, like many others before him, eventually fled for the hills. For a spell, David Patrick and I were the last ones standing, and we bore the brunt of Jill Barad's rage. By then, she seemed to have alienated most of the top management, having cultivated few allies or partnerships, a critical mistake in any corporation. My partnerships were such that if you couldn't deal with me, you could deal with Perik or Murray. And even if that proved problematic, we had our bench strength. The woman who had made the cover of *Business Week* and *People's* Most Beautiful list became an industry pariah—and let me tell you, if she was going down, she was determined to bring me with her. I was given a $5-million severance package and was required to sign a non-compete contract that prevented me from working in software or any of its peripheral industries for three years. It was like my right arm had been sawed off. I joined the exodus of former TLC staff heading for the door. Seventeen months after the celebrated deal, I left a big building holding nothing but a small box. Trailing me, and the others, were several lawsuits that were never proven out, including one for $5 billion that was hand-delivered to my home in Boston.

NEVER THREATEN, ONLY ACT

Over the next three years, there wasn't a month that would go by when I wasn't served a subpoena to appear in some beige, window-less office, opposite a line of nameless, faceless lawyers, to answer a long list questions about TLC's finances. These lawsuits were brought by class action lawyers blaming me and my team, along with Barad and Mattel's board of directors, for the failed merger. Behind the scenes, Mattel desperately tried to prove it had pur-chased a weak company that had the power to topple an industry giant. If the cases went to trial, the class action lawyers were deter-mined to wipe out my net worth. Even my own lawyer told me I might have to write a check.

I was adamant. A check would mean admitting guilt, and I'd done nothing wrong. It would mean I had knowingly handed Mattel a hobbled company, and nothing could be further from the truth. I took immense pride in helming TLC, and it had been an incredibly profitable company under my leadership. I told my lawyer I would never hand over a check, because the allegations being made simply weren't true. Unfortunately for Mattel, our former CFO, Scott Murray, had kept meticulous financial records that proved TLC's consistent performance and profitability up until it became part of the Mattel family. Murray was able to show, in black and white, over and over again, that Mattel had taken TLC, a healthy, growing company, and killed it through mis-management. Mattel, meanwhile, had misplaced its key records, a bad thing for a company trying to prove its competence. These cases were eventually settled using insurance money. Not long after, the lawyer who attempted to sue us went to jail for bribing a shareholder on another case.

After going through an experience like that—hours of interrogation, lawyers trying to pit my former partners against me, surprise subpoenas, the threat of wiping out my fortune—I no longer fear litigation. I know how the blood is chilled by an appearance of a quiet man in a dark suit, sitting in your waiting room, holding a fistful of papers. I understand lawyers, how they think and operate. Today, I never threaten litigation. When pushed, I simply sue. My experiences have taught me how to fight and win in the legal trenches. I have no fear of it now.

Mattel's purchase of TLC became a cautionary tale taught in business schools. But there is one bittersweet coda: Mattel eventually sold TLC to a company called Gores Technology for nothing but a share of future profits—if there were any profits. I consider it no small vindication that it took Gores only eight weeks to make TLC profitable again.

HOW TO BE A GREAT BOSS

Over the years, I've worked for others and I've worked for myself. Through trial and error, I've figured out a few key character traits that helped hone my leadership skills. Directness, transparency, and decisiveness are three essential traits of a good boss. It's also important to remember the rules outlined below.

1. **Employees are *not* your friends.** Even if you like them, even if you hired them because they *are* your friends, while they are working for you they are not your friends. They are your employees. The problem with socializing with your employees is that it makes it hard to be objective about their performance, and harder still to crack down on them if they're underperforming.

2. **Maintain a clear line of command.** In most of my endeavors, I've had a partner, and we've helmed our companies side by side. But I weigh in on issues that fall outside the realm of my command only when completely necessary. Employees always knew which problem to take to Michael Perik and which to take to me. Overlap of authority can get confusing, muck up productivity, and cause unnecessary delays, if not out-and-out grief.

3. **Be accessible.** You're not building a fiefdom—you're building a company. Don't alienate, isolate, or separate yourself from your partners and top earners. Don't put them on hold, don't fail to return their calls, and don't make them feel like they

cannot approach you. I've seen this phenomenon firsthand. It's toxic, and it's usually the product of fear or the inability to cope during troubled times. If your first instinct is to bury your head, you are not a leader.

4. **Delegate, delegate, delegate.** You cannot—nor should you— do everything. CEOs who think that they should weigh in on every single aspect of their company get too bogged down in the details, much to the detriment of the overall health of the company. If a ship's captain is overseeing the catering, he's going to hit an iceberg.

5. **Don't procrastinate.** When an employee is problematic, you must act. Now. Do it right. Do it by the book. But do it.

6. **Never pass the buck.** Blame stops with you. It always stops with you. Even if you think you had nothing to do with the decision that got your company into trouble in the first place, you're wrong. You likely had something to do with hiring the person who *did* screw up. Take immediate responsibility, do what you can to fix the problem, and then whack the knuckle-head who couldn't keep pace. If your name is on the product, business, or marquee, that's especially important.

7. **You're not their parent.** Employees will only bring their drama to work if you let them. If you don't want to be treated like a parent, don't act like one. If employees are having squabbles, let them figure it out among themselves. I also try to steer clear of giving personal advice. My employees' problems are

their problems to solve. And it's up to them *not* to bring those problems to work. By the way, if one of your employees is suffering from a genuine issue—addiction, depression, that kind of thing—don't suggest that they get help, insist upon it.

8. **Life's not fair.** Some people will simply make more money than others in the same job. Some people will work harder. Some will get higher sales. You will trust one over the other to get the job done. You will likely have favorites. That's life. If someone complains about it, tell him or her to get over it.

9. **The boss doesn't always make the most money.** Find stars and pay them well. If you want to attract those stars, you'll have to lure them with dollars. Remember that money's the great motivator, and if it means you take a hit financially, take it. Talent will always bring in more money for the company, and that has got to be your number-one priority always. Which leads me to . . .

10. **The company comes first.** This is the most important tenet. Having a singleness of purpose—the health and welfare of the company—keeps things clean and clear. Employees never question your priorities, nor do they have to guess at their goals.

CHAPTER EIGHT

HEAD DOWN, KEEP MOVING

FAILURE IS THE BEST TEACHER

In the weeks, months, and years following my departure from Mattel, I'd often hear Gerry Patterson's advice ringing in my ear: "Put your head down, kid, and keep moving." But for a while after that, I couldn't see beyond the end of my bed. I entered into one of the darkest chapters of my life. I now know that I'd rather invest in entrepreneurs who have experienced failure than those who think they'll hit it out of the ballpark every time. I realize now that failure helps build those aforementioned calluses. They're the marks of a tried-and-tested entrepreneur. The wisdom I've gleaned is a direct result of riding out uncertainty and bad times. Every entrepreneur will feel the unforgiving lash of failure, but I've come to see that how you handle failure is the truest indicator of future success.

The TLC sale to Mattel was one of the highlights of my professional career; the post-sale stint was one of my lowest moments; and the aftermath of the merger was, for me, one of my biggest personal failures. But even then, I never doubted that better things awaited me. I just didn't know what they were.

With my hands shackled by a non-compete clause I'd signed upon exiting Mattel, I couldn't jump back into software, an industry I knew well. Another line of work didn't immediately beckon. I was financially stable enough not to have to hit the pavement anytime soon. I had a healthy severance package, plus I still held a lot of Mattel stock that paid a nice dividend. I would

A well-needed vacation with my family.

be okay for a while. So what did I do next? I shuffled around in my pajamas for a couple of weeks. I got reacquainted with my wife and kids. Then I outfitted myself with the best cameras money could buy, told Linda to find a beach, and we booked flights for the whole family. Then we found another beach, then another one. For the next several months, we traveled around the world and I took thousands of photographs of my wife and kids, people I loved and had missed dearly. It was as though by taking pictures I was trying to freeze this moment in time, because I had the keen sense that in the blur of building wealth I had lost a decade with them. In the end, being fired, shackled, and paid to leave was a great bonus for my family. It was one of the happiest periods of our lives. It was also good to be away, because the press was merciless, accusing TLC of all sorts of nefarious actions that weren't true.

TOUGH TIMES CALL FOR GRIT AND GRATITUDE

During that period, I became aware that whatever I paid attention to grew. If I focused on the bad news and the awful aftermath, it seemed that the whole world was pointing its finger at me. If I focused on the amazing company we had created, I began to trust that I could do it again. I just had to brush myself off and get back on that entrepreneurial horse. I also had to remind myself that TLC had been the seller, not the buyer. The basic rule of mergers and acquisitions is this: once you sell a company, it's the buyer's to profit from or screw up. As the seller, my job was to maximize value for my shareholders. I had done my job.

With time, I learned to ignore my critics, because opinions hold no power or truth. They're just opinions—which are so often uninformed—and the critical chatter died down and eventually disappeared. The nattering nobodies became like the Greek chorus for a new economic bonfire. By 2000, dot-com start-ups were falling like timber in a dry forest, one after the other. It's easy to blame lack of caution and shoddy due diligence, but remember that at the time, the whole tech bubble was filled with unknowns. Few people predicted that the bubble would burst so spectacularly and so quickly, because it had been a generation or two since anyone had seen such a meteoric rise in a brand-new economy—since the invention of the automobile, the radio, or TV.

I was old enough to see that a pattern had begun to emerge in my life. After every heartbreak, every trauma, every disappointment or failure, there was always a low time. After that, my life always got better. I had no reason to believe it wouldn't be true again.

I snapped out of it. I no longer allowed myself to lament my post-Mattel life. In fact, I had to see the non-compete clause as a chance to start all over again and do something new and exciting with my life. I don't do well when I'm directionless. For me to be happy, I have to have a purpose. And I knew my purpose in life was to make money. That's why being an entrepreneur suits me so well. An entrepreneur at loose ends is an entrepreneur in the genesis stage of the next big venture. I began to set the course for the second half of my life. I was forty-six years old and in no mood to wind down. At first, Linda loved that I was home all day, shuffling around in my slippers, sipping coffee, and splitting the newspaper with her. But after a year of seeing me in a bathrobe, even she wanted me out of the house.

IF AT FIRST YOU DON'T SUCCEED, GIVE UP (THEN TRY SOMETHING COMPLETELY DIFFERENT)

My next money-making move, along with my backers from Citigroup, was an attempt to buy Atari, the massive video game company that had just launched the home-gaming companions to the Wachowski Brothers/Keanu Reeves *Matrix* movies. I loved the idea of getting into the movie-licensing business and applying it to video games. In terms of the non-compete clause, video gaming was a gray area. The work still involved computers, but video games weren't educational software, and technically they weren't toys, either. Still, the idea hit too close to home, and luckily the deal fell through—I was told Mattel was watching my every move.

After that, I hit on another venture, this time to create something called the Home Game Channel. The idea was to coalesce every video game available onto one cable TV stream. For a monthly fee of about $19.99, viewers would be able to access this giant storehouse of video games and play whatever they wanted, whenever they wanted. It was an idea ahead of its time, and I had no problem rounding up funding from high-profile venture capitalists. The gaming companies also signed on in droves. Then I took the idea to the head of one of the biggest cable companies in the U.S. He easily saw big potential in this idea. But naturally his company wanted the biggest piece of the pie: a third of both the equity and the monthly fees. After all, it was providing the pipeline that would feed the games into Americans' homes. But that percentage was a hard sell. The investors and the gaming companies thought that because *they* were providing the money and the content, they should have a bigger piece of the pie than the cable provider. My job was to work out an equitable split for all three sides: the gaming companies that owned the intellectual property, the venture capitalists who had the money, and the giant cable conglomerate that was the gatekeeper to the entire enterprise. I became a "greed umpire," trying to negotiate with all three sides so no one would lose sight of the opportunity. The giant cable conglomerate spent millions on viability studies looking into how to restructure its billing department to accommodate the demand. One leading company proposed the compromise that the venture capitalist would get 15 percent, but it didn't fly.

It's hard to watch money die on the battlefield over a bigger share of the enterprise. When a company is in its embryonic stage, greed can sometimes be a corroding force because people are arguing over imaginary dollars. In that argument, character is often revealed, and *that* can cause players to retreat. Greed is good—I believe that adage—but it can wreak havoc on fragile enterprises.

Home Game Channel was a missed opportunity. It was great that big companies now returned my calls, but I realized after my stint with Mattel that I couldn't get into business with them. It would slow down the entrepreneurial process. If I do business with big corporations now, it's only to sell them a company and move on.

After the demise of Home Game Channel, I met with Scott Sperling, one of our former TLC shareholders from Thomas H. Lee. The topic of digital-TV licenses came up, because there were a number of them for sale in Canada. Cable was exploding and specialty channels focusing on food, cars, lifestyle, game shows, politics, renovations, you name it, were all coming available. And since I was Canadian, Scott urged me to check them out. If I found something I liked, maybe Lee would fund it, he said.

BENEATH EVERY REJECTION LIES OPPORTUNITY

I made inquiries into buying Report on Business Television, or ROB-TV, the Canadian business news channel. But we soon discovered that the Canadian Radio-television Telecommunications Commission (CRTC) required that channels be 51 percent Canadian owned, something Boston-based Thomas H. Lee would never agree to because he wouldn't have control. I thought the CRTC policy was myopic, an outrage, and I said so to anyone within earshot, including Jack Fleischmann, the CEO of ROB-TV. I cold-called him from Boston, introducing myself as an independent investor. After a lively discussion, which included a provocation for Jack to put *me* on TV so that I could tell it like it was, he invited me up to Toronto. I hadn't been thinking of myself as a TV personality, but I did watch a lot of CNBC, and I told Jack that I could do better than those blowhards.

"A lot of people say that, Kevin. Why don't you come up to Toronto and prove it?"

I love a dare. A few days later, I met Jack and we talked for hours about everything from the CRTC policy and the difference between investing in the U.S. and Canada to how I interpreted the stock markets. Programming was just wrapping up for the day, so Jack threw me right in, asking the ROB-TV anchor to lob a few questions my way at the end of the show. It was an off-the-cuff audition. Jack stood behind the camera in the dark of the studio. Every once in a while, I could hear him chuckle. It was my first time in front of the cameras, my first time being interviewed, but I wasn't nervous. I felt completely at home. I immediately felt that familiar click, that sense that this was something I could do and enjoy. Why? Because I'm the same off camera as I am on. I've never felt that I had to perform. I think that's the key to making a good presentation — let alone good TV. That old cliché "Be yourself"? Well, it's true.

My first gig on the Business News Network in 1996.

After the Q and A, I got up from the anchor desk and Jack greeted me with an enthusiastic handshake.

"You're a natural," he said. "I've been doing this for a long time, and I knew in the first thirty seconds that you've definitely got something."

A TV career was born.

My first gig on the newly renamed BNN (Business News Network) was as a roving investor, the everyday guy who was managing his own money. I'd discuss what I thought of certain stocks and funds, using props like boxes of dog biscuits that I'd shake at particularly bad investments. My mandate was to be smart and honest, but irreverent when possible. This was a dry financial channel, and if I wanted people to listen, my message had to be entertaining. Remember that Don Cherry was merely *talking* about hockey, not playing it. He knew his delivery had to be as entertaining as the game itself.

Soon I was paired up on a regular basis with a smart journalist named Janis Mackey Frayer. We'd get into knock-down, drag-out debates with a little bit of name-calling and a lot of vitriol thrown in. No one had ever used words like *stupid, ridiculous,* or *moronic* when it came to talking about business, but those words regularly peppered my diatribes. I started to ask myself, "Would I say this if the cameras weren't rolling?" If the answer was yes, I'd let it rip. The phones regularly lit up.

I flew from Boston to Toronto every week to do my TV gig. Not that this paid the bills—far from it. I did it because I knew the Canadian business world watched BNN, and I wanted to be a part of that world in the country from which I came. I had been absent from the scene for more than a decade. This was a great way to announce my reappearance.

Meanwhile, the TV work was quietly rebuilding my internal scaffolding, which had been badly compromised after the battering

Me with Reza Satchu—one of my key partners.

from Mattel. It was also introducing me to a whole new pool of movers and shakers, including Reza Satchu, who would soon become another vital business partner.

EXPERTISE CAN BE TRANSFERRED

Perhaps because software was so ephemeral, ever-changing, and hard to pin down, I was eager to turn dramatically in the direction of capital acquisition—real estate—something concrete, reliable, "there." Reza Satchu was my entrée into that world. I knew nothing about real estate, but Reza had heard I was a keen marketer, and that's precisely the skill set his new venture was lacking. Reza was a young, up-and-coming entrepreneur with an eclectic background. Born in Kenya, raised in Scarborough, Ontario, educated at McGill and Harvard (where he met the mutual friend who introduced us), Reza worked in the rough-and-tumble world of Wall Street and had founded several businesses, including one that sold for more than a billion dollars. Along with his father, Rustom, and his brother, Asif, Reza was already buying up acres of industrial land across the country and converting them into storage property. His theory was that Canadians were incredibly mobile, their lives ever-changing. Divorce, job loss, promotions, and downsizing all created the need to rent temporary storage. I also realized that the ever-shrinking square footage of condos provided a constant stream of clients who needed overflow capacity for their stuff. We were riding the real estate boom of the early 2000s. People were buying property like crazy. But our company, called Storage Now, wasn't in the real estate business; it was in the "stuff" business.

As the marketer, I knew our key clients were condo owners who needed extra space. I could market to developers, who would funnel business our way. I could also speak the language of the city councilors to get the proper zoning we needed to erect our facilities. Ours was another example of a vital partnership in which each person's weakness is mitigated by the other's strength. It took us only three years to build Storage Now into a company worth $100 million, the second-biggest storage company in Canada. I was back in business. Literally.

CHEMISTRY ISN'T A MYSTERY

Meanwhile, my gig at BNN was expanding. After Janis, my regular co-panelist, left for a news-reporting gig overseas, Jack Fleischmann decided to pair me up with Brian Tobin, a former Liberal politician. Our new daily show would be called *Squeeze Play*, where the "left-wing" and "right-wing" business perspectives would duke it out over the airwaves.

Jack realized the panel would need a solid, objective news anchor to give Brian and me discipline and focus, so he hired a young business journalist named Amanda Lang. At first, I thought our fights might get ugly. What if we upset this tiny, fragile-looking news anchor? How was she going to control us? What if I brought her to the brink of tears every night? That wouldn't be good. Janis had learned to deal with me, and now I had to break in a new person. But it wasn't long before I realized Amanda was more than up to the task. In fact, she landed a few early punches that had me reeling against the ropes. (That was also around the time I learned that showing up to the set a little hungover wasn't a great idea.) Amanda and I had such great chemistry that when

Brian left after a few months, Jack never replaced him. *Squeeze Play* became our program.

Right out of the gate, I teased Amanda for being the only bleeding-heart liberal with three hundred pairs of shoes, a number she has never confirmed. She took my ribbing with class, even when I called her the most attractive "commie" on television. (By the way, she comes by her champagne liberalism honestly. Her father was Otto Lang, a long-serving Liberal MP and cabinet minister under Pierre Elliot Trudeau.) Rather than being insulted, Amanda laughed at me, and then proceeded to try to dismantle my arguments with her unassailable smarts.

People often talk about good chemistry as this unknowable X-factor. It just *is*, they say. But I don't agree. On The *Lang & O' Leary Exchange*, which I now co-host with Amanda, she and I are a great team for the same reasons that John Freeman, then Michael Perik, and then Reza Satchu and I were all great teams. We don't overlap; we don't compete; we bring different views, skills, and ideas to the table—and when those individual parts gather, they create a fully integrated whole. That "wholeness" has a certain pleasing resonance viewers can sense. Good casting agents know they can make or break a production when casting for chemistry, and in a lot of ways, that resonance is exactly what they're looking for. And when they strike it, it feels like a tuning fork hitting that perfect pitch and tone. You feel its rightness in your bones.

The other reason the TV partnership between Amanda and me works is that while we each disagree viciously with the other's opinions, we know each side of the debate vitalizes the other. Plus, I trust that Amanda has my back. This is live TV. She knows

I can be a little undisciplined when it comes to expressing myself, and she inches me away from that tricky line where passionate opinion can veer into a rant. Amanda's cool intellect counter-balances my rougher street smarts. Her bemusement tempers my ar-rogance. My fearlessness and her diplomacy make us a good match when interviewing a guest.

Over the years, Amanda has become one of the best partners I've ever had in any venture—bar none—and a brilliant foil for me. I have never purported to be an intellectual genius, but I gain credibility by going head to head with her on a daily basis.

Amanda Lang and me—a great partnership.

OPPORTUNITY IS OFTEN RIGHT UNDER YOUR NOSE

A show's greenroom can be a huge asset, when used right. A green-room is where TV guests relax while waiting to be called to the set. No one's completely sure about the origins of the term *green-room*, which was coined decades, if not centuries, before Johnny Carson and David Letterman brought cameras into those mys-terious, windowless holding areas. When Amanda and I were co-hosting *Squeeze Play*, it seemed that every hedge fund manager, politician, author, artist, thinker, blogger, and CEO wanted the same thing: to be on the show. And if they came on our show, they had to spend time in our greenroom. I began to greet guests there before the show. I'd warm them up if they were nervous, and sometimes I'd just catch up with old friends. Those off-the-record conversations have yielded some incredible ideas.

During a brief conversation with a famous media personality we'd booked on the show, the subject of bonds came up. I told her I was poised to buy a specific family of media bonds that had been trading quite high after a rocky season. She suggested that I wait until the forwards were published. (A forward is a list of companies committed to advertising in a certain publication over the next ninety days.) It was an offhanded suggestion, providing insight about how she invests, but I took her cue and called my guy to tell him to hold off buying the bonds. Sure enough, four days later, the forwards came out and they were bad. I saved a fortune that day.

I began to use whatever fame *Squeeze Play* allotted to me as a way to reinforce my investment style, to paint broad and fine strokes that fleshed out my political, financial, and philosophical bents. People interested in doing business with me knew where I stood and, more important, how to find me. I no longer had to chase down deals; they came to me. I was beginning to garner a few perks for being recognized for *Squeeze Play*. I'd get noticed in restaurants in Toronto's financial district. Strangers would buy me a drink or email me to say they agreed with something I had said the day before. Still others wrote to tell me I was an asshole. Mostly, it was flattering nonsense that I didn't give much thought to. I wasn't famous. But I did begin to understand that if I didn't figure out a way to seriously monetize this TV hobby, it would have to go. TV took too much time out of my busy day—time I needed to spend making money.

TEST YOUR APPETITE
FOR CHANGE

I'm a man who loves change. For me, sameness equals stagnation, and stagnation equals the death of opportunity. We began this chapter in the depths of my post-Mattel despair, after which I dusted myself off, invested in a completely different asset class (real estate), and made my name in a brand-new industry (television). But change isn't easy, and it isn't for everyone. If you want to be successful, as an entrepreneur or as a rising star in your company or industry, you must embrace change and sometimes be the agent of it. Test your tolerance for change by answering these questions with *always, usually, sometimes, rarely,* or *never.*

1. When my company introduces a brand-new computer program/ phone system/inventory-tracking device, I am the first to sign up for tutorials on how to master it.

2. I like when our company goes through an internal reshuffling process. It keeps the staff fresh and prevents the kind of entrenchment that can suffocate productivity.

3. New bosses or co-workers take getting used to, and I'm the first to show them our protocols and to be available to answer questions and concerns they have about the company.

4. I'm happy where I'm at, but I always keep one eye on other possibilities, not only within my company but also with our

competitors. Updating my résumé is something I do every few months, because you never know. I don't like to get too comfortable.

5. What seemed like a great idea or policy yesterday fell apart upon implementation. I like to cut my losses, undo the decision, and try something else immediately.

6. New corporate acquisitions can cause massive upheaval. I find those chapters of any business to be stressful but invigorating. Uncertainty sometimes breeds new levels of creativity, inspiring innovations and uncovering solutions you couldn't see before.

7. Speaking of volatility, corporations that don't stay limber will not make it through unscathed. Rather than wait in fear, I like to figure out ways to empower managers, ensuring they have the latest tools and remembering to always keep them in the loop about impending policy changes.

8. Even during massive shifts, there are things you *can* control: spending, staffing, and security. I keep a tight leash on those departments and ride out the rest.

9. Market fluctuations are par for the course. When I invest, I'm in it for the long haul, and even if my portfolio takes a major hit, I'm aware that selling off stock isn't the best way to recover and rebuild. The markets reward perseverance, consistency, and persistence—never more so than in times of change.

10. I try not to be locked into policies that begin with the words *never* or *always*. Because you never know. Things always change.

If you answered *always* to all of these scenarios, you may be a bit *too* amenable to change, possibly to the point of being inconsistent or a tad flighty. Try to find a balance between *always* and *usually*—a nice sixty-forty split feels right. I'm not a big believer in all the new age–speak about "coping with change" and "communicating your feelings" around change. You can get stuck in a sort of inert emotionalism. Instead, tackle change like a realist. Know it's the only constant. Don't get mired in thinking about, anticipating, and fearing change. Simply accept it and make your next move. Here's an old adage to live by: the way to be safe is never to be secure.

CHAPTER NINE

LEARNING TO BREATHE FIRE

MONEY DOESN'T BUY YOU EVERYTHING

I love TV. I *get* TV because, like me, the camera never lies. If you're boring, TV shows it. If you're defensive, angry, stupid, or dull, TV lays those traits bare. Despite the rise of the Internet, TV is still a very powerful medium. It has an incredible reach, it opens doors, it gets your name out there, and it can be very exciting.

I was on the set of *Squeeze Play* when Stuart Coxe, an executive producer from the CBC, called to see if I'd like to try out for another TV show, this one about venture capitalism. It was called *Dragons' Den*, he said, and was a Sony reality-TV franchise already airing on the BBC in the U.K., where it was immensely popular. I made a mental note to check it out on YouTube later that night. Stuart went on to describe a rather odd-sounding concept: five wealthy venture capitalists sit on corporate thrones and weigh in on business ideas that entrepreneurs bring to them—one after the other. If the capitalists like the business, they can invest. But the catch was that they are investing for real—with their *own* money. The Dragons, as they are called, are told nothing in advance about the entrepreneurs pitching, except their names. Stuart explained that he'd have to do a background check on me to make sure that I was rich enough and legit enough to participate on such a panel.

"I've seen you on BNN," he said. "I think you'd make a great Dragon."

Maybe. But this show sounded risky. Bad enough to stumble on BNN, a small specialty channel with a niche audience. The CBC was an institution with broader reach. Being part of an upstart business-reality show on a network not known for that genre, about an industry not known for its entertaining qualities, seemed risky. Plus, I'd be spending my own money on any venture I took on. Besides, did I want to be known as a "Dragon"? My soldiers were barely out of the hospital. Could I justify sending my money back into battle in front of an entire country? It didn't seem all that appealing.

Furthermore, what did these earnest CBC types know about finding investment opportunities? What did they know about venture capitalism? What kinds of businesses were we going to see? A parade of llama farmers looking for start-up capital to expand their sweater lines? Basement inventors hoping to recoup Grandma's cash, which they'd already sunk into some useless, stupid gadget? (Actually, we see a lot of those.) It could be a gong show of epic proportions, assuming anyone even watched the thing. Then again, I thought, money does have the power to bring on theatrics. It could be entirely genius.

"What do you say?" Stuart prodded.

"I'm in."

The Dragon auditions were held in the slick, cavernous studios on the top floor of the CBC building in downtown Toronto. The producers threw out a wide net in their search for potential fire-breathers. But the main criterion to be a Dragon seemed to be wealth. If you were rich, you got a call. The parking lot of the CBC was an exercise in automotive one-upmanship. I pulled up in my Porsche, only to be flanked on one side by a Lamborghini driven by a handsome young guy with vivid blue eyes and a really bad tie, while on the other there was a Russian billionaire and his $500,000 Mercedes McLaren, driven by his bodyguard.

The audition greenroom was like an elite cocktail party, except the party thinned out as each candidate was cut. TV producers are merciless types. They may look like harmless academics—the guys with their rumpled chinos and women with their comfortable shoes—but let me tell you, they're bloodless vipers.

For three days, thirty of the wealthiest business luminaries in Canada were trotted out and tested in various combinations. Each had submitted to a background check, and each had to ensure they had at least $250,000 to spend on new ventures. Some were people I knew; some I had never heard of. Each could buy their way in and out of any gig—except this one. Either you had the chops for TV or you didn't. For a show like *Dragons' Den*, you also had to be able to talk about money and the world of venture capitalism in a way that didn't baffle or belittle the audience.

Over the course of three days, I was one of a few candidates left standing. I was called back to sit next to other Dragon hopefuls to see how our chemistry matched. At one point, Stuart sat me beside an Internet security millionaire named Robert Herjavec, the handsome guy with the Lamborghini . . . and a full head of hair. To get acquainted, I teased him about his tie. Sure, he looked like a young Robin Williams, but looks weren't everything, right? Could he hold the audience's attention? The producers seemed very interested in seeing what this Herjavec fellow could do in front of the camera.

They brought a test entrepreneur into the soundstage and placed him right in front of Robert and me. The pitcher was asking for an exorbitant investment in exchange for a tiny slice of a nonexistent business. Before he could finish the first minute of his pitch, I started in on the guy about his numbers, launching into the kind of diatribe a real entrepreneur would receive if he wasted a venture capitalist's time in the real world. I couldn't help it—and when Robert smelled blood, he joined me. We were like lions cornering a gazelle. By the time we were done with the guy, there was nothing left but a pile of smoking bones. That's when a spark ignited; something about our dynamic brought a bit of life to the room. I began to see that this crazy show might actually make really

The inaugural lineup of *Dragons' Den*, 2006. Left to right: Robert Herjavec, Jim Treliving, Jennifer Woods, Laurence Lewin, and me.

good TV, because talking about real money always has a way of drawing out real emotion. Everyone wants more money, and most people are afraid to ask for it. Here was a show that captured that agonizing process.

A few days later, the producers had whittled the potential Dragons down to the final five for season one: cattle millionaire Jennifer Woods, food giant Jim Treliving, the late great lingerie mogul Laurence Lewin, Robert Herjavec, and me.

GOOD IDEAS GET YOUR ATTENTION— GREAT IDEAS GET EVERYONE'S ATTENTION

Shooting began a few weeks later in an abandoned factory in a rough, undeveloped part of Toronto called the Distillery District. It has since become an arts and culture hub with acres of restaurants and condos, but at the time the neighborhood was rather rustic, to put it kindly. Stuart explained that the producers didn't want *Dragons' Den* to feel corporate. They wanted the show to take place in surroundings that were tactile and real—where things are *made* and work is *done*. This was about entrepreneurship, after all, and it wasn't all clean and pristine. Later, I learned that the producers also wanted to have some distance from the CBC. Rumor had it that many people in the building, including some of the higher-ups who originally okayed the production, were worried the show was going to be a massive failure. In 2006, reality TV was considered a grimy genre, beneath the lofty mandate of the nation's venerable public broadcaster. Not a year earlier, the then head of the CBC, Robert Rabinovitch, had testified at a Heritage Committee hearing that he would never put a reality TV show on the CBC schedule. A year later, *The One*, CBC's attempt to duplicate *American Idol,* epically tanked. Even some of the technical crew from that show refused to work on *Dragons' Den* because they didn't want to be associated with yet another bomb. Many of the production crew running around that first day consisted of freelancers brought in from outside companies. But I knew none of this at the time. I thought it was all a lark. I was excited.

I arrived at the crack of dawn to a full-blown production in high gear. The set was teeming with lighting specialists, sound technicians, makeup artists, jib operators, carpenters, caterers, and a massive truck that pumped in cool air between takes. It was *Squeeze Play* times a thousand. The energy was palpable. Pitchers were corralled in the hot tents like nervous cattle. My fellow panelists occupying the makeup chairs were tense, too, and a little skeptical that this thing would fly, but, hell, we all were up to the challenge. We were from different backgrounds. Almost from the get-go we did not see eye to eye on things. Jim, Robert, Jennifer, Laurence, and I had made our fortunes in very different ways, after all. But we had one of the most important qualities entrepreneurs must possess: a passion for spotting fresh opportunities.

The first few pitchers sent down the stairs were practice runs for us. They didn't have viable ideas or real companies, but Stuart wanted us to cut our teeth and find our groove. My first indication that we were onto something special was when I noticed that the crew really paid attention to the proceedings. They even began to act like the audience. During breaks, I'd overhear them pulling apart our reasoning about why we'd trashed an idea or why we'd taken a risk on some new venture. As a former cameraman, I remembered how indifferent crews often are about the production they're working on. They're hired hands. Their job is to light, shoot, and record. Because of the technical demands, they often can't concern themselves with the content, the actors, or the general goings-on. That's the job of the producers and the director. But during the *Dragons' Den* shoot, the crew was rapt. From the sound and camera people to the makeup artists and gaffers—they all paid attention to the pitches and passionately discussed them around the craft-services table over lunch.

For the rest of the day, we started to have some fun batting around the silly ideas some of the pitchers proposed, biting into a few good ones, making what we thought was a little TV show that might garner some attention from business geeks before quietly disappearing forever.

Even early on, there were several interesting pitches—nothing like the stellar businesses we see now, but I was quite intrigued by Ginch Gonch, a saucy underwear company with an insane valuation. After the arrogant president turned down my aggressive offer for 51 percent of the company, I made a dire prediction about his business. As he exited the set, I said, "You're a dead man walking."

Here I'm holding up a pair of Ginch Gonch, inspected by the underwear king himself, the late great Laurence Lewin of La Senza fame.

It was a mean thing to say. After the pitcher exited the soundstage, the crew remained mute. Here was a guy brave enough to launch this crazy underwear venture, and in front of several hot models, I called him a future failure. (As it turns out, the company filed for bankruptcy a year later, before an investment company bought what was left of it.) I figured if the producers were offended by my statement, they would cut it out. At the break, Stuart came over to my chair. I thought he was going to scold me or tell me to temper my statements.

Instead, he said, "That comment—'dead man walking'?"

"Yeah?" I said.

"More of that, please."

So from then on, I let it rip. The camera loves honesty, so I gave it. Stupid ideas were given a tongue-lashing, brilliant ones were aggressively pounced on and scooped up.

Then, a few days into the shoot, four students in matching orange ties descended into the Den. We knew instantly they were bringing something special to the table. They were barely out of their teens but had created a clever website devoted to minimum-wage jobs in the fast-food and retail industries. Finally, a real idea with the potential to be a big business. Jim Treliving and Laurence Lewin were ready to put their whole enterprises into their system, a massive opportunity for everyone. All five Dragons were on board for $200,000. But these students needed guidance and mentorship, so even though they came offering only 15 percent of their company, after some haggling, our final offer was for 51 percent—a controlling interest. The students hesitated, then agreed. We really wanted to help them, beyond throwing big business their way. We shook hands. As they left the Den, I said, "This could pan out."

Jim added, "We'll see in due diligence."

A few days later, the shoot wrapped. There were some con-gratulations and back-slapping. With the footage "in the can," as they say, the five of us dispersed and went back to our lives, none of us thinking we'd really see each other again. We thought we had just shot this lark that might be exciting for entrepreneurs in Canada, but beyond that, who would watch?

NEVER TAKE ADVICE FROM DILETTANTES

In October 2006, *Dragons' Den* premiered to dismal numbers—a little more than 200,000 people tuned in. A bomb. Stuart Coxe sent out an apologetic email titled "Oh Well . . .," thanking everyone involved and reminding them that at least we had some fun—at least we tried. But every week, the ratings kept climbing, until the finale, eight episodes later, which would feature the disastrous conclusion of the JobLoft deal.

Almost immediately after the Den handshake with the kids from JobLoft that day, we deployed a team of lawyers and accountants to go through the students' financial statements. Miraculously, JobLoft breezed through the due-diligence process. While the show was airing to tepid ratings, we got ready to cut them the check for $200,000, and booked the handover shoot to take place in Robert Herjavec's office overlooking Lake Ontario. The scene would close the season's finale, due to air in a couple of weeks.

After we settled in around a massive board table, we soon discovered that the students had been receiving advice from a behind-the-scenes player—their business professor. He not only sat on the board of JobLoft, but had some definite opinions about how we planned to market the website and who its intended audience was. He stood at the head of the table, the ink not quite dry on the $200,000 check, and proceeded to launch a hail of insults at the people bringing real money to the table—the

Dragons. It was fascinating to watch this academic, this dilet-
tante, hijack the proceedings, the camera following his every
move. For twelve minutes, he wrote a bunch of numbers on a
board, presumably to demonstrate to a guy like Jim Treliving,
a man worth millions, how to run a business. After a while, I
tuned out what the man was actually saying, paying attention
instead to how his arrogance and ignorance seemed to suddenly
drain the lifeblood—and the money—right out of the room.
Still, this man held us rapt with his assertion that our $200,000
investment was rather "measly." It was mesmerizing. I had so
many responses stacked up in my head. I wanted to ask this professor: Are you crazy? Have *you* ever invested almost a quarter
of a million dollars of your own money in a business dreamt up
by teenagers? More important, have you ever had the incredible
privilege of making other people wealthy? Or, conversely, have
you suffered the awful, sinking feeling that comes with losing
your or other people's money on a bad deal or investment
because you weren't careful, because you leapt before peeling
back all the layers of the company you were courting, because
your piece of the pie wasn't proportionate to your risk?

The students just sat there, blank as fish. That they weren't
embarrassed by their professor's insolence, his utter lack of respect
for our commitment to fund them, actually depressed me. Then
the professor asked us Dragons if we had business degrees. I
replied, "What does it matter?" But Robert, a self-made millionaire who had earned every penny in the vicious trenches of
Internet start-ups, had had enough. When the professor made a
jab at Jim for flying to the meeting on a private jet, Robert leaned
over, snatched up the check, and ripped it into tiny pieces.

Robert, ripping up a check and killing the JobLoft deal.

If I had been one of those students, I'd have launched myself across the table and stopped Robert. I would have said, "Wait! Don't kill the deal! Don't kill the money! We can work this out!" But their passivity told us everything we needed to know about those young men and who their key influences were going to be—not their shareholders, not their investors, not even the money, but rather, this professor and his untested theories. It was an implosion the likes of which I'd never seen in venture capital history. The money ran screaming from the table. It was a disaster.

YOU CAN'T MANUFACTURE WORD-OF-MOUTH MARKETING

But it wasn't a disaster for the Dragons. The lifeblood—the essence of business, the force itself—is the cash. Deals can walk away, but we still had the cash, and that cash flowed safely elsewhere, multiplied, and did good things. More important, that crash and burn was some of the best reality TV ever produced about the world of business and venture capitalism. It demonstrated that this little show, *Dragons' Den*, was the real thing, that the money was real, and that it could change lives in real ways. The cameras captured the fact that money had the power to bring out the best and the worst in people, and that it was infinitely fascinating to watch. Word about this little TV show—where money could meet tragic or triumphant ends—spread like wildfire.

The check-ripping hit YouTube, spreading overseas because people in far-flung countries have even stopped me to talk about it. Before that episode aired, ratings were uneven, rising and falling a little every week; another season was not assured. After it aired, our ratings doubled to about 400,000, ending the season on a very high note. Shortly after, we were renewed for a second season, during which the ratings climbed steadily, averaging about half a million by the last episode. In the third season, we hit a shocking one million viewers by Christmas, increasing our audience share by 350 percent, in particular with the most coveted of all demographics—viewers between eighteen and twenty-four years old.

Today, *Dragons' Den* brings in some of the highest ratings for the CBC, regularly peaking at more than two million viewers by the end of each airing, and some weeks even besting the ratings behemoth *Hockey Night in Canada*. As of this writing, we're the number-one Canadian show, our reach extending to one in three households in the country. Incredible. But I can pinpoint the moment *Dragons' Den* was transformed from a specialty program into a ratings juggernaut. It was the moment Robert Herjavec ripped up a check, a *real* check, for $200,000 on national television, proving that money rewards you when it's respected, when it's treated properly—and that means not only when it's deployed but also when it's kept safe.

Not long after *Dragons' Den* hit that million-viewer mark, the CBC hired Amanda and me away from BNN, launching *The Lang & O'Leary Exchange*, our daily business show that analyzes the market and puts decision makers on the hot seat. (People sometimes ask me why our program isn't called *The O'Leary & Lang Exchange*. For one thing, Amanda is actually one of the producers of our program. The other thing is, I am nothing if not a gentleman.)

MAKING TV (AND MONEY) IS CONTROLLING CHAOS

Going into season two of *Dragons' Den*, we had to find a new female Dragon, after Jennifer Woods bowed out. It's not easy to find a charismatic businesswoman who's not only smart, rich, and telegenic, but can hold her own in a den full of male egomaniacs . . . and me. Mike Armitage, one of the show's producers, combed every financial publication and made calls to every Bay Street insider in search of one such woman. He found a few stellar candidates, and I tested with all of them. But when he found Arlene Dickinson's name and her company, Venture Communications, at the top of a list of the best-run companies in Canada, he picked up the phone. He asked her if she had ever heard of *Dragons' Den* (many of the candidates still hadn't). He was quite relieved to know that she had not only heard of it but was a fan.

"Why do you ask?"

"Because I think I'm about to change your life."

Arlene was sent in to test, and I liked her right away. She had the right balance of toughness and "kumbaya" warmth. Plus, she had terrific style—that vivid red hair with the dramatic white streak. There was no contest. Since joining the Dragons, she's proven to be savvy, sexy, and wise, and has become one of my most formidable allies—and competitors—in the Den. Arlene has since joined a long line of women, which includes my mother, my wife, and Amanda Lang, who can tell me to shut up without suffering many repercussions.

Arlene Dickinson and me.

Then, tragically, during the hiatus between seasons two and three, Laurence Lewin succumbed to cancer. He was a true Montreal *bon vivant* and an incredible wit— beloved among the crew, production team, and audience. I really can't say enough good things about the man. What you saw on camera—the humor, the wry observations, the kindness, the sheer fun he had—that was all real. Plus, he was a human calculator, moving numbers around in his head with incredible speed and accuracy. He is still greatly missed.

The producers never set out to replace Laurence—an impossible notion, anyway. Instead, they looked to cast someone who could bring a similar energy, with a different view of business. Being good with numbers was a bonus. They found it in spades with Brett Wilson, an oil-and-gas magnate from North Battleford, Saskatchewan, by way of Calgary. We disagreed about a lot of things, on camera and off. In fact, we couldn't have been more different. But I respected Brett's success, and during his three seasons on *Dragons' Den*, he certainly embodied that entrepreneurial spirit that makes the show a hit.

In the world of high finance, days start early—as they do in the world of television. As chairman of an investment fund company,

I'm in the business of interpreting chaos; in television, we manage it. I have no trouble going back and forth between TV and high finance. In fact, each world keeps me sharp for the other. But like high finance, TV chaos isn't really chaos at all. It's actually a carefully controlled series of decisions, which starts with the audition process.

Like migratory birds, every spring, intrepid CBC producers fan out, setting up tables at chambers of commerce, shopping malls, and schools across the country. And every spring, more fresh, hopeful entrepreneurs line up to try out for a spot on *Dragons' Den*. Some pitches are serious; some are strictly entertaining. But even the serious ones require sprucing up in order to pass muster in the edit suite. To make the television show work, you need a mix of funny, fierce, lucrative, and lucky. You also need to throw in some surprises. Who would have thought a couple of women hanging from the drapes would score a deal? But that's exactly what happened on the third season.

It was September 2007. *Dragons' Den* had become a bona fide success, delivering steady ratings and ad revenue. The quality of the deals we made with pitchers had gone up, but so had the "wacky factor." I have a lot of patience for a good spectacle, but season three brought a pitch that really began to define my Dragon persona, and Brett Wilson's as well.

Aerial Angels, as the two acrobats were called, had auditioned through the *Dragons' Den* website. The producers quickly saw that their idea to make a traveling show out of their acrobatics would make great TV and called them in for the shoot. The set was cleared so that they could set up their props. We came back from a break to a giant tripod with what looked like red drapes suspended from its center. Two athletic-looking women entered the den. After a lively demo, in which an acrobat hung and spun from long red drapes, then ate some fire, the founder of the troupe presented her business plan. She wanted $200,000 for 20 percent of a national tour. Presumably, the box office earnings would pay back the initial investment and earn some money. I had a small problem with her business plan in that *she did not have one.* I also wasn't terribly impressed with the acrobatics. Worse was the fact that she talked over everyone, making it difficult to get a word in edgewise. She was arrogant, and I told her so, and that's when the tears fell. There she stood, bawling on national television, apologizing for being unprepared and pushy. I was unmoved. While Arlene handed her a

Arlene wasn't thrilled about me scolding one of the Aerial Angels for crying on the Den. But tears and business don't mix.

Kleenex, I said, "Money and tears don't mix. Get over it. Life's hard. Money doesn't care. Your tears don't add any value."

Brett, however, *was* moved, to the tune of $250,000, which he ended up giving her for half the company. That money went on to finance their road show, and though Brett likely hasn't made a dime off the investment, that moment solidified him as the Knight in Shining Armor, and it certainly reinforced that I was the Mean One for making her cry. I have been a vocal critic of that deal, accusing Brett of being unable to differentiate a charity from a business. And I still feel that that segment should have received an R rating—parental discretion should have been advised—because it sent the wrong message to children: "Come on TV and cry and you'll get some money." Kids, that is *not* how business is done!

After six seasons and more than a thousand pitches, I am continually in awe of the parade of hopeful entrepreneurs who show up every year to dazzle and entertain. Sometimes, I completely forget that cameras are filming the proceedings, and that there are twenty very tense TV people sitting in a dark control room a few metres away, watching every conceivable angle. Talking about money has a way of crystallizing the moment to the exclusion of everything else. I think that's why *Dragons' Den* makes such compelling TV. We really are riveted by the spectacle unfolding. When you see us impressed, it's because we really are engaged or completely bowled over by a business idea or opportunity. Some days, it's like a private talent show has been put on for our edification, and I feel like a Tudor king with a giant gong. Here, before us, are people willing to travel across the country and risk humiliation and pain, all in the name of making money. I love that I have front-row seats and even get to play a role in the proceedings. Television is the most interesting hobby I've ever had. And thanks to the *Dragons' Den*, it's becoming lucrative.

My real job is chairing a company that manages a billion-dollar family of funds, but I look at it this way: where O'Leary Funds is science, television is art. As a frustrated artist, I can't think of a better combination to balance out both sides of my brain than the way my life is structured today. I make room for both TV and high finance because each, increasingly, requires the other. My funds earn me a seat in the Den, and the Den keeps me flush by featuring opportunities for investments, or by simply broadcasting my investment philosophy.

FROM THE DEN TO THE BOARDROOM: HOW TO PRESENT THE PERFECT PITCH

During the shoot, I am usually the last Dragon to stroll in, around 7:30 a.m., sometimes after a rowdy game of squash. (I learned on that trampoline in Montreal that I need to exercise to prep my brain for long periods of concentration.) While my head is being powdered, a producer gives us a broad rundown of the day, during which we'll see anywhere between ten and twenty pitchers. That's far more than the average venture capitalist will see in a day, but whether you're prepping for a TV show or to present in front of a board of potential investors, the number-one rule is to make your pitch incredibly dynamic. Below you'll find a few pointers. These reflect my own opinions on what works, what doesn't and why. This is advice any entrepreneurs can use before they make that big, important presentation.

1. **Keep it simple.** Make sure you can explain your business to an eight-year-old. The producers on the Den are *not* business experts; they're in the business of making a TV show. If you think the Dragons are impatient, you haven't met the average reality TV producer. No offense, but they have the attention spans of gnats. However, most venture capitalists will concur that if it takes more than a couple of sentences to explain the opportunity, the idea probably needs more polish. So prep and practice. Get it down to the bare essentials.

2. **Keep it lively.** If you're talking about a dry business, like security software or an agricultural product, you must find creative and entertaining ways to demonstrate it, or you will not make the cut. We love to see all kinds of businesses, and the producers make every effort to throw viable ones our way, no matter the class or category. But you must then make every effort to turn your presentation into a production worth watching and enjoying. Think of it as though you're putting on a show . . . and the venture capitalists are clutching invisible gongs. And believe me, if you think I'm vicious in the Den, try boring me in my own boardroom. I get much grumpier.

3. **Watch the show.** You'd be surprised by how many people vying to be on *Dragons' Den* have only ever *heard* of the show, and decided to audition upon their family or friends' urging. Very dumb. The show is everywhere. The CBC website has an archive of virtually every episode. Watch and learn. By the same token, know everything about the business people to whom you're pitching. Get the prospectus; read the web site; Google the hell out of them. You'd be surprised at how many people think they can simply "wing it."

4. **Keep props to a minimum.** On the show, every single prop has to pass muster with the show's director. She has sweeping authority to put the kibosh on your elaborate graphics, your life-size mannequin, your comprehensive PowerPoint demonstration, or anything else that might clutter the shot or make it difficult for her camera to get the angles. No amount of begging will change the director's mind. If she hates your

poster, it's toast. (Posters should also have a matte finish, or on the air they'll look as if you're standing in front of a big piece of glass.) Just as in real life, there's a big difference between a solid pitch that happens to dazzle and one that needs to dazzle to hide its lack of substance. Remember: less is usually more. If yours is a good idea, it won't need bells and whistles to make the grade.

5. **No entourages.** Don't show up with your Aunt Betsy who's a big fan of Jim. The greenroom is small, the days are long, the food's bad, and the producers are cranky. There is no live studio audience, no backstage area, and no closed-circuit feed to watch the goings-on in the studio. The *Dragons' Den* shoot is expensive, fast-paced, and intense, so there's no time for visits, viewing, pictures, or wandering. And in real life, if you've got several partners who all want to make the case to potential investors, keep the cast to a minimum. Bring only key players. For my money, I need to have the CFO present because all my questions will concern money. VPs can usually wait in the car.

6. **What not to wear.** Don't wear anything white, busy patterns, hats, costumes, or distracting garments that haven't been approved by a producer. We shoot in the winter and air in the summer, so dress accordingly. Shorts look stupid on TV in November. In fact, your terrific little pitch could hit the cutting-room floor because of the way you look. Same goes for making that crucial first impression. Dress the part of a winner—whatever that looks like in your chosen field.

7.   **Be safe and practical.** Remember, it's a long day. Bring some-thing to read and something to eat. And in order to get to the Den, you have to walk down a pretty treacherous flight of stairs. Keep that in mind when choosing footwear. No one's fallen yet, but you don't want to be the first. That's a scene that *won't* likely hit the cutting-room floor, and I've always wondered if the producers are hoping for a small, painless slip to happen.

8.   **All numbers on the table.** Nothing bothers me more than when entrepreneurs want to keep some of their numbers off the record. You must be prepared to disclose *all* relevant information, no matter how succulent the margins, how big the profits, or how many competitors you fear might be watching the show. Put your figures on the table—on TV and in the boardroom—all your figures, period. Or stay home.

9.   **Do your own PR.** If you are selected to be on the program, you won't get much notice, so be prepared to launch your own media blitz. Gather local media contacts, write yourself a press release, then hit Facebook and Twitter like crazy. Big and small businesses are increasingly required to be social-media savvy. You must have some facility with Facebook and the like; it's the new "shorthand."

10. **Get ready to fill orders.** More than two million people could see your pitch if it's aired on the show. Two million. So stock your product, update your website, and man the phones. After the Holy Crap cereal pitch aired in season five, the

company's website crashed within minutes. Orders came in so fast and furious, the local post office in Sechelt, British Columbia, had to hire four new people. Mistura makeup had the same sales boost in season four. If you get on the show, you're not only pitching your product or business, you're launching it. Again, it's all about being ready, not just for your pitch or presentation, but for what happens right after you nail it. You must be able to hit the ground running and follow through on all that great promise.

CHAPTER TEN

THE ART AND SOUL OF A GREAT PITCH

THE PERFECT PITCH: A GREAT STORY WITH A HAPPY ENDING

The producers of *Dragons' Den* are fond of saying, "We're not making a business show that happens to be on television. We're making a television show that happens to be about business." This is a key distinction. In other words, no matter how lucrative the deal, it will not make it to air if it's boring, if it lacks the essential ingredients that make unforgettable television. Each pitch must tell a story about money: the lack of it, the need for it, and how it can be made. As a born marketer and avid salesman, I tell my employees all the time: if you cannot tell the story and put your prospective customer into the narrative of our financial products, you will fail. Good TV is no different from good storytelling. That said, the success of *Dragons' Den* hinges on the show's ability to fold serious businesses into a compelling narrative.

On *Dragon's Den*, I would say, without hesitation, that almost all pitches are blown in the first ninety seconds. Some people come dressed like bozos, which happened in season five. An entrepreneur had an interesting enough idea, an online repository for students to rent used textbooks. But he came out dressed like his company mascot, a yellow lion (Jim Treliving thought he was a sunflower), and I ripped him apart. There's room for irreverence in irreverent pitches. But he was asking for serious money for a serious venture, and he was dressed like he he'd just stepped away from a kids' birthday party. He misread the room. Still, his mistake did make for some memorable TV. And no, the producers tell me that they did not put him up to the stunt. Apparently, the lion costume was his own bad idea.

On TV, and in real life, we're dealing with real ideas, real businesses, real capital, real investors, and hopefully, real deals. But it's infinitely harder to pitch on TV. There are a thousand lights, long waits, imposing cameras, bossy producers, heavy makeup, and cavernous soundstages; and after that gauntlet, nerve-racked entrepreneurs must face down five fierce and seasoned business experts who are often in vicious competition with one another. So it's very intense. And it only takes ninety seconds to screw up the whole thing. I'll break down exactly why that first minute and a half is so crucial, whether you're a pitcher on the show or you're pitching to a prospective investor anywhere. Most often, entrepreneurs don't get a chance to know what the investor is thinking, what he or she is looking for, so I'll try to let you in on the things I look for (and these are things that many, many venture capitalists out there are also looking for).

The first thirty seconds of a pitch are intuitive, visceral, from the point of view of the investor. I watch the way the pitcher enters the room. It could be the look in a pitcher's eye, the spring in her step, the color of his tie, the style of her shoes, the tangibles and intangibles of personality that make me lean in closer or sit way back. Maybe the pitcher reminds me of some-one from my past—someone I liked, or didn't. But I can tell instantly whether I even want to hear this entrepreneur's story. And make no mistake: that's what all pitchers are here to do. They're here to tell me a story—one with a happy ending that involves how I can make some money.

Over the course of the next thirty seconds, the pitchers intro-duce themselves and the opportunity. Are they poised and con-fident? Are they meeting my eye? Are they mumbling? It's understandable if they're a little nervous, especially if they're on set, but there's a difference between shyness and neurosis. I look for that difference. After all, this is someone who's going to con-vince me my money won't be put in harm's way. The best pitchers are like brave lieutenants coming to borrow my soldiers for a battle they know they can win. If they show up sweating bullets and stam-mering, with no plan of attack, I'd be sending innocent monies to slaughter, a crime for which I should be court-martialed.

The final thirty seconds gives me the dollar amount the pitchers are looking for. I want to hear how much pitchers think they're worth, so that figure can bang around inside my head while they describe the opportunity before me. An interesting alchemy hap-pens in the brains of most entrepreneurs. Say an entrepreneur asks for $50,000 for a 10 percent share. This person is valuing their entire company at a half a million dollars. If they unveil a shoddy gadget held together with spit and duct tape, with no sales and no business plan, I'm going to be a little perturbed. What they're saying to me is this: Look at this amazing idea I have. Can I have a reward for thinking this up? Instead of paying close attention to the rest of the pitch, I start batting them around like a bored cat trapping a tired mouse. That's what I do to people who waste my time. It's worse when they have a terrific idea with no sales. Suddenly that half-million-dollar valuation is blocking my ability to see the real opportunity. It acts as an unfortunate blind spot that undermines credibility, hobbling the rest of the pitch. On the other hand, a realistic valuation—say, $50,000 for 10 percent of a company that manufactures a line of gloves that protect manicures (and look stylish to boot)—that's something I can get behind. And did—on season four of *Dragons' Den*.

When the women from Dig It Handwear entered the Den, the air was immediately charged with their competence and pro-

fessionalism. Both were smartly dressed in attractive business suits and heels. They had a brisk gait, an inoffensive ask, followed by a clean and concise explanation of their product. Because they were already selling the gloves, they could prove that the market was interested. There was cash flow. Next, they articulated exactly why they needed the money. They

Me with one of my favorite investments, Dig It Handwear, moments after we shook on a deal in the Den.

were going to produce an infomercial for strategic markets in Canada and the U.S. They had plans to expand their line of products. They also had an exit strategy, and could list a number of companies that might want to eventually buy Dig It if they started to carve out market share with their niche gloves.

By the end of that crucial ninety seconds, they had told me exactly how their product worked, what was in it for me, and why I'd get richer. By the time they wrapped up their short, well-choreographed demonstration, which was both instructive and compelling (it involved Arlene digging around in a little flower garden), they had produced that elusive *aha* moment that comes when entrepreneurs solve problems you didn't even know you had. I was sold. They were wise to have chosen Arlene for the demo. They knew that if they could sell her on the glove's key feature — cushioned tips that protect your manicured nails — they'd sell the rest of us. After all, the gloves were made for Arlene's demographic.

Each moment of that pitch built to the next, generating power and force, like a symphony with a joyous conclusion. I couldn't help but be swept along. There was no resistance. Turns out, our enthusiasm was well founded. As of this publication, the gloves are in Canadian Tire and Home Hardware, and sales are through the roof. In 2009, they did $90,000 in sales. In 2010, sales were $259,000, an increase of 287 percent, with projections for 2012 in the $750,000 range.

EXECUTION IS EVERYTHING

Let's say an entrepreneur aces the introduction, articulates the opportunity, produces a terrific demo, and outlines a competent business plan. Next, I ask myself: What about this entrepreneur? Does this person have the ability to execute? Can I ride this pony for a whole cycle, or do I have to whack the rider because he or she can't execute this great idea I've fallen in love with? Good ideas are easy to come by, great ideas less so, but execution is everything. These are all things that are going through my head during a pitch. That's why I like to own control, or 51 percent, just in case the guy I rode into town with isn't leaving with me. I can whack him and put in a better manager. Maybe he'll still maintain some equity, that's fine, but the whole thing's about execution. I want a doer in that job, not a dreamer or a talker, and quite often, opportunities dry up because the entrepreneur who gave birth to this great idea is too ego-driven, too single-minded, or too scattered to pull it off.

Then there are the true champions, that rare breed of born entrepreneurs. They have all of the above elements, with an added power: the ability to withstand a barrage of questions. Here are the types of questions you're likely to face on *Dragons' Den* and in the real world of venture capitalism:

- What would you do if things went wrong?
- What would you do if your market share suddenly slipped?
- How much does it cost to advertise your particular gadget/business/service?
- How much inventory do you have to build?
- Do you plan to franchise, or can you license the concept? Do you understand the difference?
- What were the margins in the first year? Second year? Third?

- What were your profits in the first year? Second year? Third?
- How much capital do you require? Where would you deploy it effectively?
- How flexible is your manufacturing plan? Any resistance to taking it overseas? And if so, why?

Given my own experience, you can perhaps understand why being able to answer every single one of these questions is crucial, and why successful entrepreneurs can provide solid answers while unsuccessful ones can't. I am held to these standards all day, every day, and so should be the people in whom I invest.

If you watch *Dragons' Den*, you'll see that when entrepreneurs understand the questions and give answers that are consistent with their vision, they get a deal. Almost always. Because to maintain composure during that kind of barrage, to produce solid answers and a satisfying conclusion, tells me that they value my time, and that this idea—this business—matters to them more than anything else. They sold me on them. And *that* tells me there's a chance my money will be safe.

KNOW YOUR NUMBERS: ALL OF THEM

The single biggest mistake entrepreneurs make when they come to me for my money is not knowing their numbers. What do I mean by numbers? Here are just a few that you should know like your own name:

- What are your gross margins?
- What percentage of the market do you have to capture to break even?

- I'll assume you know your profits (see above), but what profits have your competitors generated?
- Where is it cheaper to produce your product?
- How much are your retail listing fees?
- Will those fees likely go up or down?
- How much interest is on your debt?
- How much debt are you in to begin with? (You'd be surprised how many people don't know this number.)
- What percentage of the company is yours?

If you can't answer *all* of those questions, it tells me one thing: I can't invest. My money won't just be unsafe—it'll be decimated. So as soon as somebody starts bumbling the numbers, I'm gone. As a pitcher, you have to know your numbers the way you know your name, phone number, and birthday. And if you don't, you're just "the vision guy." No big deal if that's your role. But you have to bring somebody who *does* know the numbers. Otherwise, you'll be whacked, and not just by me. I've seen Brett and Arlene, both considered the "nice" Dragons, rip pitchers wide open for the

Jim's an ex-cop, so this is a duel I'd likely lose.

crime of incoherent numbers. It's fun when that happens. I feel like I can sit back and take a little break.

I've gone in on deals with every Dragon, and Robert and I can often see eye to eye on proposals. But the Dragon I'm most in sync with is Jim Treliving, who's a value-yield investor like me, and who, like me, partners with shrewd bastards who watch their bottom lines like scurvy hawks. I admire Jim. Under that cuddly exterior is a true financial Dragon.

THE TRUTH SAVES MONEY—AND LIVES

Let's say you have a great idea. You may even have the beginnings of a good business. But when you want to give me only a 10 percent cut of the business, it's insulting. There was a doctor on season five of *Dragons' Den* who, I admit, invented a terrific little gardening gadget. It was a blunt plastic tool that you pressed into the earth to make a perfect hole for planting. He asked for more than $300,000, yet offered a mere 10 percent to us Dragons. In addition to taking a risk with an unknown product, in a finicky market, we were supposed to help him secure clients, market the product, find distributors, build and store inventory, and pay retail listing fees. Keep in mind, his demand meant that he was valuing his one-product company, which had so far sold nothing and generated no profit, at $3 million. Needless to say, I couldn't jump on board.

Why do people overvalue their companies? They have access to the same metrics as any entrepreneur. I think they lose all sense of proportion because they've been locked in a basement with an idea for too long. Like Dr. Frankenstein, they've fallen in love with their monster, making it impossible to see its flaws and defects.

That kind of driven myopia makes it hard for their loved ones to be honest with them, so often the first time they're receiving constructive criticism—the brutal truth—is when they're facing me and the other Dragons. And they're shocked—*shocked*—to learn that an idea with no sales—completely untested in the marketplace— simply isn't worth anything. When pitchers on the show ask for a giant sum of money for an idea that has made not even one penny, I have been known to call them greedy little pigs. Maybe that sounds mean, but I hope that now that I've explained things, you can see there's some truth in what I say. But here's the thing about pigs: almost all of them eventually get slaughtered.

MONEY AND EMOTIONS DON'T MIX

Another big mistake when it comes to pitching is over-sharing. For some reason, pitchers feel I need to know their medical history, their family's troubles, their dead dog's name, and the fact that their girlfriend dumped them days before they met me. Here's the thing: I don't care. I blame this trend on some of my more sentimental colleagues on the show. They have contributed to making our business environment conducive to that kind of pap—but it's a waste of my time. Every once in a while, a pitcher commits the cardinal sin and crosses the line from emotionalism into full-on crying. That's when they lose control of the pitch, and everything falls apart at the seams. I've seen it happen countless times. I find it distasteful. It shows your weakness and it makes my money cling to my pant leg.

When it comes to the art of making money, the only currency outside of the cash itself is speaking the truth about business. Comforting someone who's sunk a chunk of their family's fortune into a ridiculous venture, as some of my fellow venture capitalists on TV do, is the true crime.

Season five brought us a real heartbreaker, an elderly woman who should have been enjoying her retirement, but was instead brushing off an old (bad) idea and pitching it to us as a revolution in eco-hygiene products. She had invented flushable toilet seat covers that would sell in vending machines in public washrooms for a whopping two dollars. It was an awful product, with an awful business plan and an awful demo—her elderly friend had pinned a bunch of vile words to his pants to demonstrate the kind of detritus you could find on a toilet seat: *poo, pee, STDs*—you get the picture. But the real tragedy was that she had sunk more than a million dollars of her own money into this venture. This money was spent in noticeable increments— over a twenty-year span—so I was left wondering who in their right mind let this woman slowly and tragically go completely broke. Why did no one stop her? I was not only out, I called it a stupid idea and ordered her to stop pursuing it, immediately. Some of my fellow Dragons were angry with my tone, but I stand by my intervention. Some people really need to hear the truth, and it's much meaner to let them continue to deceive themselves and risk financial ruin than tell them straight up to stop their madness.

When you tell the truth to people, when you tell them to stop spending money on ridiculous ventures, stop investing other people's money and their own on a dog of an idea, it's deeply satisfying work. Because every once in a while, *it* happens: the light comes on behind their eyes. The truth can cause a financial spiritual awakening. Suddenly, the person realizes: "This idea *is* a dog! I *have* wasted time and money on something that will *never* work. I have to stop. Now. Kevin O'Leary has saved me from ruination."

These entrepreneurs may leave in tears, but because the lives of innocent monies have been saved, their families won't be out on the streets, and they can comfortably retire or move on to more fruitful ventures—or even to a solid, well-paying job. Far from guilty, I feel utterly exhilarated by telling it like it is. That's why I call myself Mr. Wonderful, even when some of my fellow Dragons call me other things entirely.

INVESTIGATE THE FINANCIAL, THE PERSONAL, AND THE CRIMINAL

So you've made your pitch and the Dragons have fallen in love with the product, the plan, and the possibility. The handshake moment you see on TV, after a brilliant pitch comes to a successful conclusion, often feels like an ending, and a happy one at that. But it's really the beginning of a rocky and rarely rewarding chapter. In the real world, less than 10 percent of handshake deals ever close, and the Den's no exception. People often think that after the Den goes dark, we call in the lawyers and accountants, draw up a shareholders' agreement, shake again, sign, then toast to future success. But there's a whole other process that takes over after we've shaken hands, one that lasts longer than forty minutes. It's called due diligence, and it can take weeks, months, and even years. It's when the hard work really begins for any partnership between a pitcher and an investor. That's when both sides engage in a no-holds-barred investigation of what all parties are *really* bringing to the table.

Let's look at the women from Dig It Handwear. During the due-diligence process, the first thing I checked for was whether either of them had ever been to prison. I'm not kidding—you'd be surprised how often that pops up (but fortunately not in this case). We did a background check, delved into their credit history—because everybody has a history, a paper trail, or baggage. Even I have baggage. I expect potential investors to investigate me, and I expect them to have a string of questions I'm always more than happy to answer. In fact, I wear the scars of my experiences proudly. It's important to be forthright and lay all your dealings on the table, because evasiveness means the love affair's over. If something's fishy about the income statements—*poof!*—the deal dies. If I smell any rot or the opportunity looks bruised, I dump it. Especially if the entrepreneur is making any attempt to hide problems or paint over them.

After I weigh their legal baggage, we move on to the next process: revenue, cash flow, the numbers. I want to know if the numbers they presented on air were accurate. Did they truly reflect what they had promised during the pitch? Were the profit margins exactly as described? Here is where you begin to feel whether a story holds together. You have to think of due diligence as though you're peeling the skin off an onion. At the first sign that things are not what they seem, deals fall apart. During pitches, people sometimes exaggerate, they get caught up in the moment, or they outright lie. Why? The pressure, maybe, or they just get caught up in wishful thinking. They want to believe they're as successful as they claim they are, so their numbers are more reflective of fiction than fact. It's not just bad business practice, it's a lot of damn work, because you have to remember everything you've lied about, and continually retrace and recover your steps. It may be hard to resist the temptation to exaggerate your projections, or to cover up a bad credit history, but don't do it. You will be discovered. So cough it up from the get-go. You never know; your honesty might still get my money. Always remember: truth is your friend in tough times.

Sometimes, deals that die in due diligence break your heart. I still think fondly of the Uno from season four, that futuristic unicycle invented by Ben Gulak, the smart-est teenager in Canada. He wanted to mass-market his zippy electric vehicles, selling them in traffic-clogged cities like Beijing first, before bringing them to North America. All five Dragons fell in love with the young man and the plan. We shook on a deal that would give him $1,250,000 for 20 percent—an astonishing amount, but fully worth it if this vehicle could be fine-tuned and mass-produced. But during the

Ben Gulak, the creator of the Uno.

due-diligence process, I became concerned that the Uno's two-wheel design might encroach on other intellectual property in this area. This is not an uncommon dilemma for technology ventures—but it's one that could take years, if not decades, to sort through, so I backed out. (By the way, Brett is still backing this young man, who's making his mark at the Massachusetts Institute of Technology. I predict we'll hear more great things from him in the future.)

In some cases, an idea *seems* sound, but very often a pitcher hasn't road tested the idea outside the confines of a supportive circle of friends and family. But a good nose will detect that nearly indiscernible stench that's at the core of every single bad venture: exaggerated projections, shady business partners, insecure patents, cooked books, intractable debt, and saturated markets.

Sometimes, I back out of a handshake deal based solely on personality. How a pitcher moves through due diligence tells me everything I need to know about whether to move forward. A few more minutes in an entrepreneur's presence, and you realize he or she is someone you cannot work with. You find out they're sniveling, whiny people who can't take the heat. Or you feel that they don't have the stamina to move confidently forward. After a little TV attention, suddenly they're under the misapprehension that you're best friends, or that they're worth a lot more than they really are. They get greedy and up their valuation. You don't see these character defects until you actually sit down and do business with them. Sometimes, they're under another misapprehension: that you're going to work very closely with them to help get their venture off the ground. That's not how it works. With some exceptions, writing a crucial check is usually the only effort I'm willing, or able, to exert. I do mentor entrepreneurs if their business is closely aligned with mine. And I did make an enthusiastic cameo on the Shopping Channel for Dig It Handwear. But those women run that business and simply keep me apprised of how it's doing. I don't interfere unless I'm utterly convinced it's necessary. I invest in people who can take it from there, competently, passionately, and profitably.

As an investor, I believe it's plain idiocy to put money into the hands of somebody who vacillates or equivocates, because that's often someone who can't execute the business plan. I may still like the business. I may have fallen in love with the opportunity. I may even go ahead and invest. But in that case, I'll whack the entrepreneur, and fast. Remember, viewers see six, eight, ten minutes of footage on a TV show. And even though the show is edited and pitchers have had more than double that time to pitch, it still isn't long enough for me to know for sure whether I want to be in business with them. After all, the people with whom I've just shaken hands will not just be cashing my check; they'll also have my phone numbers, and they'll be privy to my schedule, my colleagues' schedules, and perhaps my clients' schedules and contacts, as well. I also haven't met their partners, their clients, the people with whom they do business. There are so many variables, so many reasons why, in the end, I might walk away from a handshake deal. I don't doubt my decisions when I walk away. I've never had regrets, no matter how well these businesses end up doing without my money. When I walk away, they are dead to me — gone. I move on to the next potential venture in front of me.

KNOW YOUR DRAGONS

Pitching for an investment on *Dragons' Den* isn't all that different from pitching in the real world of venture capitalism. You have to prepare, book your appointment, bring your presentation props, and stand before one, two, or five people and make a convincing case for cash. *Dragons' Den* pitchers have an advantage, though: they can watch the show and see a spending pattern unfold. Here's an entirely unscientific cheat sheet for the other Dragons on the show, with some helpful hints and my opinions about how you might get each of them to fund your venture:

1. **Arlene Dickinson.** Arlene always says that a great gadget or product is worth zero if nobody knows about it. And she's right. She'll pounce on a business with a weak link in its marketing profile. Good marketing can't save a crappy business, but it can send a solid one into the stratosphere. So if she offers to swap marketing services for equity, you might be wise to consider it, especially if you know those costs will be high. Getting the word out doesn't come cheap. If Arlene's a partner in your company, you'd better believe she'll do (and spend) what it takes to increase awareness of your product— and in the long run, taking a slice of marketing services instead of cash might end up being a bargain. She also knows what it's like to be a single parent, making ends meet while trying to grow a business. She understands the sacrifices it takes. When she sees tenacity and life experience in a pitcher with a great idea or product, more often than not, she'll back

that person. Leave the self-pity at home, though. That's not how you appeal to Arlene. And never exaggerate your claims or tweak the facts. She has a highly sensitive BS detector. When it goes off, you have a few crucial seconds to flee the Den before you go up in flames. I'm not kidding.

2. **Robert Herjavec.** No one likes a good gadget more than Robert. Especially if it has anything to do with cars. He's a savvy tech guy through and through. But if you don't have a business plan, watch out. This is a man who came to Canada with twenty dollars and a dream. For Robert, safe-and-sound finances trump insanely cool gadgets every time. He does have a soft spot for a good sob story, and famously backed a loan for a Niagara farmer rather than let him give up any of his land. I still say that was a travesty—showing a Dragon doling out a loan on national TV. But it's not my money he's giving away. The other thing about Robert is that he cannot fathom excuses. His philosophy is "If I can do it, so can you." I don't necessarily agree with that. Some people are born entrepreneurs, and some people aren't. But the minute you start into excuses about why you haven't made this call or fine-tuned that aspect of your business, Robert will launch himself at you like an attractive but deadly missile.

3. **Jim Treliving.** I love watching Jim champ at the bit over a potential franchising opportunity or new food product. Where he goes, I'm apt to follow. Because here's the thing: like me, he's frugal, and that's the highest compliment one businessperson can give another. He's all about costs and getting them down.

And he's rich because of it. But if you stand before him with a business you think is ready for franchising, you'd better be damn sure. Your existing business needs to be dripping cash before you think of risking it all on opening more. And if you don't know the difference between a license and a franchise, here's a basic rundown: a franchise is usually a clone of its parent company, duplicating trademarks, logos, layouts, and recipes. A license agreement is a lot looser, leaving the entrepreneur with more freedom and leeway to grow a business. There are other differences, but just do your homework before you stand before Jim. He's a master at both models, but he needs to know you understand what you're doing.

4. **Brett Wilson.** At first glance, there didn't seem to be any pattern to Brett's spending. He has given money to comedians, criers, custom-home builders, and clothing retailers—including a West Coast seamstress who outfits Elvis impersonators. But there is one constant with Brett: he invests in passionate people who truly believe in themselves and their business ventures. Every single person who shook Brett's hand at the end of a pitch had a stirring tale to tell and moved him at a very deep level. Unlike me, he lets his feelings figure into his financial decisions. Brett tirelessly promoted the show and his role in inspiring the entrepreneurial spirit in this country. It was a full-time commitment for him, and it showed in his prolific deal making. Oh, it did help if you were from Saskatchewan.

5. **Bruce Croxon.** It remains to be seen what kind of Dragon Bruce Croxon will be. He's got an eclectic background, making his

millions as a co-founder of Lavalife, which changed the dating scene in Canada forever. As long as he's a good collaborator when I need him to be and he stays out of my way when I want to go it alone, we'll get along fine.

Remember, you have to know your investors, their styles, tastes, personalities, track records, and what moves them to spend. Do your research. And just because one investor turns you down, it doesn't mean another one won't see the opportunity. We've proven that on *Dragons' Den.*

CHAPTER ELEVEN

THE MESSAGE IS THE MEDIUM, AND THE MEDIUM IS MONEY

WHEN OPPORTUNITY MEETS EXPERIENCE, MAGIC HAPPENS

It was the fall of 2008, and the call came when I was in downtown Boston, heading to a meeting with hedge fund managers to get the lay of the land during the U.S. banking crisis. I still split my time between the U.S. and Canada, and I sat on a few boards headquartered in Boston.

The woman on the line had a British accent.

"Hello. Is this Kevin O'Leary from the Canadian *Dragons' Den*?"

By the end of the third season of *Dragons' Den*, the show was becoming huge in Canada. I'd started to have all sorts of strange encounters with both fans and foes, so I was reluctant to affirm her question. "Who is this?" I asked.

She continued.

"If this is Kevin O'Leary, I need you to get to Logan Airport immediately. There's a ticket to Copenhagen waiting for you at the British Airlines counter."

"What? Is this a joke? Who are you?"

"I can't tell you anything except that we need you in Copenhagen tomorrow."

She instructed me to take out a pen and write down a cell phone number. I was both alarmed and intrigued. Part of me was thinking, "What an incredibly interesting proposal." Another part was hoping that a deranged fan or disgruntled pitcher wasn't planning some elaborate ruse to take me hostage. What the hell? I hung up and called the number. After a bit more subterfuge and a curious conversation, it became very apparent that I was speaking with someone high up at a production company hired by the Discovery Channel in the U.S. She explained that her company wanted me to do a screen test with a young man named Basil Singer, a quantum physicist based in London, for a new show they were producing.

"What's the screen test for?"

"I can tell you only that it's for a documentary series that will be one of the most expensive ever produced."

"Well, I can't just get on a plane to Copenhagen. I have a job. I have a wife and kids. I'm not doing this."

"Oh," she said, "I think you will."

Click. She hung up. I stared into my BlackBerry for a few seconds. How totally insane! I immediately called Linda and told her about the phone call.

"Are you going to go?" she asked.

"Damn right I am."

Fourteen hours later, I found myself in the lobby of a rustic hotel in Copenhagen, being introduced to Basil Singer, a punk-rock-professor type who'd received similarly cryptic instructions. We were met by a couple of tense people and some expensive camera equipment. We read from a script studded with environmental terms, ad libbing when prompted. After about twenty minutes, we were put back on planes, no wiser about what we had been doing there.

Moments after arriving at Logan Airport, while retrieving my luggage, I got another call instructing me to stop, turn around, and fly back to London to test with an American environmental engineer named Jennifer Languell.

"No. This is insane. I can't just hop back on a plane. I have a job. I have a wife and two kids. I'm not doing this."

"Yes, you are."

Twelve hours later, I met an equally baffled Jennifer, with whom I did another reading from more of the same kind of script. After a spell, a producer exited from the shadows of the set to shake my hand.

"You've got the job," he said.

That was it. I'd finally had enough.

"What job? What are you talking about? Can someone please tell me what the hell I'm doing here?"

He explained a premise for a television show, one that sent shivers down my spine—not just because of its scope, but because it seemed to synthesize my entire life in one year-long venture: my childhood experiences traveling the globe, my educational background in environmental studies, my professional experience as a global investor, and my passion for photography. The Discovery

The Discovery Channel's *Project Earth*, with Dr. Jennifer Languell and Dr. Basil Singer, in Greenland, where we wrapped glaciers to prevent global warming from melting them.

Channel was producing an epic documentary series involving an engineer (Jennifer), a scientist (Basil), and an investor (me), searching the world for the ten best ways to reverse global warming and save the planet. It was called *Discovery Project Earth*, and it wasn't some wifty "greenvention" series. This was the real deal. We'd be inspecting large-scale geo-engineering infrastructure projects. We'd see the kind of ideas at which investors would want to throw serious money. My role was to see beyond the science pizzazz to find out whether we could profit from these projects.

"Are you interested?" the producer asked.

"Hell, yeah!" I said.

So began the next eleven months of my life, during which I was able to spend only seven weekends with my family. It caused huge strife, but it was a remarkable privilege appearing in a nine-part documentary series with the production values for which the Discovery Channel is known. Basil, Jennifer, and I traveled to more than a dozen countries, met with some of the world's top scientists, and were privy to some of the most incredible environmental experiments being conducted on the planet. We traveled by boat to witness a project that shot salt flares into the atmosphere, forming synthetic clouds that could block harsh rays, preventing the sun from further warming the earth. We hiked across Greenland, just above the Arctic Circle, to meet scientists wrapping glaciers and ice caps in giant reflective blankets to prevent fresh water from melting away. Then there was the mass reforestation project that involved launching small rockets carrying sapling trees out of airplanes and lodging them into the earth below, which would be not only quicker but cheaper than conventional reforestation methods.

These inventions were all brilliant, innovative, and interesting. But no matter how well they worked to reverse global warming, they'd never get off the ground in any real way until they proved they could also generate profit. There is no more important endeavor than saving the earth, or finding alternative energy sources, or preventing the annihilation of delicate ecosystems. But any green idea that can't generate real jobs and earn big profits won't last. Altruism and capitalism must go hand in hand, and there was no better example of that than the Sleipner gas field.

I'll never forget our trip out to the futuristic rig that juts out of the North Sea off the coast of Norway. The ocean made round ripples as our helicopter landed on its platform. Security was incredibly tight; few civilians had ever visited there, but we had been given special dispensation.

There we saw, firsthand, how the Norwegian energy company Statoil separates deadly carbon dioxide from gas, pumping toxic CO_2 back into the seabed instead of polluting the air with it. While the scientists and engineers geeked out over the technology, I began my financial probe. My first question: how is this billion-dollar project funded? Turns out that Statoil is owned by the people of Norway, and it has become a huge cash cow for the country. A manager explained it's funded using publicly traded bonds, which are protected against inflation and guaranteed by the gas field's assets. In other words, the funds are a safe, long-term investment that will only steadily increase in value, regardless of inflation.

On deck at the Sleipner gas field, a hundred miles off the coast of Norway.

"I want to invest in this," I said.

That's precisely when the next chapter of my life unfolded. The idea for O'Leary Funds was born on that icy North Atlantic outpost. One of my first funds, launched eighteen months later, was called the O'Leary Global Infrastructure Fund, and it was loaded with steady, long-term bonds tied to real assets—just the way the Sleipner gas field is financed. That project was the very essence of green innovation—it provides energy, reduces the carbon footprint, and is profitable to boot.

GET IT IN WRITING

Before launching the O'Leary Funds, I received another life-changing phone call. Shortly after the Discovery Channel shoot wrapped, Mark Burnett—the famed executive producer of *Survivor* and *The Apprentice*, among other television institutions—was looking for his own set of financial Dragons for ABC's version of *Dragons' Den*, called *Shark Tank*. Another plane beckoned, this one to Los Angeles. I was put up in a fancy hotel and awoke to the sight of yellow tape surrounding the pool and police fishing a dead body from the deep end. A guy had smacked his head, fallen into the pool, and drowned—the victim of too much partying. Good morning, L.A.!

My interview with Burnett was supposed to take half an hour, but it stretched into two hours. We had a wide-ranging discussion that touched on everything from the difficulty of maintaining a healthy relationship when you're always on the road, to the challenges of raising children in the digital era, to finding and working with the right business partners, to how money has a way of changing everything. He proved to be one of the smartest, most interesting people I've ever met. I left feeling that I wanted to be a part of *Shark Tank*.

Meanwhile, Burnett had also approached Robert Herjavec, having seen the two of us on *Dragons' Den*. A few weeks later, we both flew out there for the shoot. Or so we thought. The night before we were to begin filming, Burnett summoned his five Sharks to a swanky restaurant to introduce us to one another. Leaving my hotel that night, I had to step over a couple going at it in the hallway. Good night, L.A.!

The pre-shoot dinner was held at the kind of place where food is sculpted, not cooked, and you never leave the table full, because in California, you're encouraged to exist in a state of functional starvation. I love L.A. It keeps me hungry—in every way. When Robert and I arrived at our table, we soon realized that there were actually six Sharks, not five. I asked Burnett why he decided to add an extra Shark.

"One of you is actually going home tomorrow," he said.

With that, he wiped his mouth and left us blinking at each other. It was like *Survivor: Shark Tank*. Mark Burnett is a visionary and a viper—my kind of guy—but I've come to understand that his ruthlessness isn't cruel. He's icily focused on making his shows the best they can be. Feelings have little to do with making money, or making TV (which is not to be confused with being *on* television—that requires a lot of feelings).

I decided to make the best of the dinner, because it was entirely possible that I'd be on a plane back home the next day. I sat next to an attractive Shark wannabe who, when she discovered I'd appeared on several seasons of Canada's version of the show, asked if she could pick my brain.

"Sure. Shoot," I said.

She proceeded to launch into a series of questions about litigation risk, due-diligence obligations, and contractual law.

"Wow. You don't get it," I said. "This is *television*."

The next morning, she was whacked while sitting in the makeup chair, and she was on a plane back to New York before noon. Goodbye, L.A.!

Los Angeles exists in a parallel universe to the rest of the world. It's a glittering circus of epic strangeness—overrun by scam artists, nutbars, and sociopaths—and I love everything about it. But I have a policy that helps me steer clear of danger: I don't believe anything anyone tells me in L.A. I get everything in writing. If you live by that rule down there, you might make it out alive.

The next day, Robert and I made the cut, along with Daymond John, a very smooth negotiator who, like me, started his business, FUBU clothing, out of his basement. Also chosen was Kevin Harrington, a pioneer in the infomercial industry and a hugely influential voice when it comes to retail concerns. Rounding out the panel was Barbara Corcoran, a real estate mogul, a sharp competitor, and a wickedly funny woman.

It was awkward at first, getting used to this new dynamic after having worked with the same Canadian Dragons for several years. But I had no doubt we'd find our groove. In a way, when you're part of something like launching a new television show— or any venture where intense people are working closely together in a high-stakes environment—you bond like soldiers in the trenches. Regardless of how you feel about your comrades-in-arms, you've been through something profound together, and that creates a connection.

We taped season one of *Shark Tank* at the MGM studio, on the same soundstage where *The Wizard of Oz* had been shot. We were told the set had incredibly high ceilings to accommodate the flying monkeys scene from the film. We shared a commissary with the crew shooting *Iron Man 2*, and between takes we caught glimpses of Robert Downey Jr. heading to his trailer. Wandering the backlot, I couldn't help but think back to all the detractors, all the people who warned me about getting involved with a show like *Dragons' Den*. Many of my fellow financiers told me I'd make a fool of myself, and make a mockery of venture capitalism, by appearing on a sleazy reality show. These are people who would now probably trade places with me in an instant.

Swimming with the Sharks in 2010. From left to right: Jeff Foxworthy, Daymond John, me, Barbara Corcoran, and Robert Herjavec.

It soon became clear that I was the "mean one" on *Shark Tank*, cast to deliver the cold hard truth. Canada has not cornered the market on knuckleheads who've mortgaged their homes, sold their assets, or cashed in their retirement savings to fund really bad ideas or ventures. There is no shortage of pseudo-entrepreneurial Americans needing a wake-up call. But as with *Dragons' Den*, every week I'm also blown away by some of the cleverest gadgets, services, industries, and ideas I've ever seen. In season one, I made an enthusiastic bid for a company that sold course notes online to college kids; sadly, I lost out to Barbara Corcoran. And I was really impressed by a business that made patented slipcovers for those grimy playpens in daycares and schools. Come to think of it, Barbara stole that one from me, too.

On the season finale of *Shark Tank*, Robert and I aggressively colluded on a technology company called JumpForward. It makes software that allows college coaches to attract top athletic talent while still remaining compliant with the Byzantine recruitment rules that underpin amateur sports in the U.S. But my favorite deal was the one we did with Marc Furigay, an idealistic teacher from Chicago who struggled to get his students to fall in love with Shakespeare. When he set the Bard's famous plays to rap music, the kids suddenly got excited about Elizabethan English. He wrote a catalog of Shakespeare-themed songs and founded a company called Classroom Jams. He came to us for $250,000 for a 10 percent stake, which caused a feeding frenzy among the Sharks. After an emotional back and forth, all five of us came in for the whole company, paying Marc a 5 percent royalty. He balked at first, not wanting to throw the song rights into the mix, but I made the argument that without a nod from an educational publishing giant, his idea was worthless. And I was the person who could introduce him to leaders in that field. Finally, he agreed, and we all shook hands.

Like *Dragons' Den* in Canada, *Shark Tank* started low in the ratings and climbed steadily. And as with *Dragons' Den*, those who did watch became passionate fans. They filled blogs, websites, and online forums with talk about the show. I told my fellow Sharks that American audiences would need to get accustomed to the jargon on *Shark Tank*, as had been the case with *Dragons' Den*, but when the audience got hooked, they'd really get hooked.

American network executives tend to make decisions based strictly on numbers, but every once in a while they'll take a gamble on a show with good buzz. After months of meetings, we were finally given another season on ABC to prove that *Shark Tank* could be just as successful in the U.S. as *Dragons' Den* has been in Canada. The second season brought some changes, which I think only added to the show's appeal. Mark Cuban, the billionaire sports impresario, and comedy mogul Jeff Foxworthy were rotated into the Tank for a few episodes, bringing with them considerable star power and fierce competitiveness.

I'm often asked if there's a difference between the American and Canadian shows. Ultimately, the pursuit of capital and the freedom it affords looks the same on both sides of the border. In both countries, there is a healthy audience that loves to watch people ask for money. But there are two key differences to keep in mind. One, the U.S. market is bigger and more competitive; therefore, the due-diligence process is more involved because of the far higher likelihood that a directly competitive or similar product already exists. No matter how proprietary a product is, it must be checked and double-checked. I have often found five other people doing the same thing, or close to it, as the pitcher standing before me, who has assured me up and down that theirs is a unique product on the American market. Two, the banking systems in each country are very different. In the U.S., the recent economic crisis has made it difficult for entrepreneurs to secure loans they would have had no problem qualifying for a few years ago. That makes my role as a Shark a little more potent. I can make or break a deal in the U.S., whereas in Canada, a no in the Den doesn't mean cash is impossible to come by.

FAME IS A CURRENCY: SPEND WISELY

Americans understand fame as a modern-day form of currency. And even if Americans didn't invent reality TV, from *Dancing with the Stars*, *The Real Housewives*, *Jersey Shore*, and *American Idol*, they've certainly perfected it. And where Toronto might

There is always good chemistry between Daymond and me.

be all about work, and New York about the money, L.A. is ground zero for fame. It's the currency, language, and soul there.

While shooting *Shark Tank*, I get to hang out in L.A. with Daymond John, one of my fellow panelists. He also writes books, he's on the radio, and he hangs out with famous musicians who wear his clothes. Every moment Daymond's awake, he's thinking about branding and marketing. He's thinking about new ways to get the word out there about his products.

I've watched a sea of people part to let Daymond and his entourage behind a velvet rope in an exclusive club. I was invited along one night and saw the effect his fame has on the people around him. It's palpable. They *ooh* and *ah*, whisper, and point. But Daymond is someone who knows how to direct fame. He deflects it away from himself and toward the celebs wearing his clothing. And he keeps a keen eye on what the young club-goers are wearing—and not just what they're listening to, but what they get up and dance to. He knows that fame, much like money, is an energy that has to be harnessed.

Fame infuses whatever it inhabits with a certain kind of power, so it must be very carefully, very expertly employed. Hollywood stars know this. Consider George Clooney, who knows cameras will follow him around relentlessly. He makes sure they are following him to war-torn regions such as Darfur, where he can draw attention to the plight of refugees. Sean Penn manipulated the media to bring attention to the plight of Haitians displaced after the earthquake. You could argue that one of the first megastars to harness the power of fame was Elizabeth Taylor, who changed the minds and hearts of people when she began to raise money for AIDS research in the '80s, which was not a very popular cause prior to her campaign. She was a great woman.

In L.A., I can see how fame can be corrosive, undermining the very people it once blessed. You hear about all the toppled starlets who tip off paparazzi to their whereabouts for a little attention and cash. TV and film are intoxicating environments, and it can be fun to be recognized. But if you look to fame as a one-way street, designed only to get you attention, you risk becoming a caricature, your fame folding inward on itself. Think of those reality-TV brats from *The Hills*, Heidi Montag and Spencer Pratt. They're cautionary tales in L.A.: full of regrets and silicone. On the other hand, Lauren Conrad, their co-star, played it smart, using her fleeting moment in the spotlight to spin out a million-dollar fashion-and-style brand that extends to books, clothing, and a website.

I'm old enough to understand the toxic underbelly of fame, and I'm glad I never had it when I was young. I don't overindulge, I eat well, I exercise, and I take care of those I love. Fame is fun, but it's fleeting. As of this printing, *Shark Tank* is a cult hit in the States, and I still travel freely without being constantly recognized. But when *Shark Tank* becomes as big in the U.S. as

A party broke out moments after the last frame of *Shark Tank*, season one, was finished shooting on the Sony Pictures lot in L.A. in August 2009.

Dragons' Den is in Canada, it won't change me. I'll know what to do with that additional attention. I'll simply use it to make more money.

Here's a great example of how I do this. Before *Shark Tank* hit the airwaves, the promotions department at ABC asked me to fly to a taping of *Dancing with the Stars*. The task was to attend the show and, on a commercial break, say into the camera,

Me and my fire-breathing friend.

"Watch *Shark Tank* on ABC, after *Dancing with the Stars*." Now, I love ABC, and I love *Shark Tank*, but nothing in me wanted to fly eight hours for an eight-second promo hit—until the publicity agent told me I'd be sitting next to Steve Wozniak. Wozniak, along with Steve Jobs and Ronald Wayne, was one of the founders of Apple Computer. I'd fly very far to sit next to Wozniak. Why? Because I had a lot of questions, and he doesn't give many interviews. I got to the taping, made a beeline for the empty seat next to Wozniak, and then did my bit for the ABC team. When I had him alone, I told him how much I loved Apple, but that I couldn't own the company's stock because it doesn't pay a yield. He asked, "Why don't you investigate the Asian chip manufacturers? They all pay yields." The next day, I did just that, and eventually moved a good chunk of cash into those companies. So you can see how an eight-hour trip for an eight-second hit can help me build my fortune. That, to me, is the real power of TV.

But I don't use TV to advocate for causes or charities, not just because it isn't good for business, but also because charities change. That said, I donate a portion of my wealth every year. I give quietly, employing a method I call "Five for Five." For five years, I focus on five charities, giving them each the same amount of my money. After five years, I reassess. Sometimes I continue my support for one or two causes, folding in a few new ones. Sometimes, I find five new causes, whether they be in the arts, education, health care, or international relief. That's how I believe wealth is best employed. Make a lot of money, then give a lot of money to the people, causes, and charities that can best put that money to work.

Whether I'm wearing the scales of a Dragon or the fins of a Shark, my message is consistent and clear: I want to go to bed richer than when I woke up.

By reinforcing that idea on my television shows, in books, on the radio, and in newspapers and magazines, I've made making money my brand. And it's working. At a recent road-show presentation for O'Leary Funds in Newfoundland, an investment adviser told me that when he informed his client he was going to see me, the client said, "I just hate that man. But I want to invest in O'Leary Funds."

HOW TO MANAGE YOUR PERSONAL BRAND

Make no mistake: if you have a Facebook account, a MySpace page, a Twitter profile, you are a brand. Every time you upload a photo, add a link, or post an update, you're putting into the world another idea of yourself and what you stand for. These are innovations built to harness an innate quest for fame, marketing, and promotion, even among your own circle of friends. Here's the thing I tell my kids, who've grown up with digital technology: you will be Googled—not just by some guy in chemistry class with a crush on you, but by every prospective employer you will ever have, for the rest of your life. Keep that in mind the next time you post those photos from spring break in Cancún, or if you're considering getting that LIVE FREE OR DIE tattoo on your inner forearm. Anything directly associated with you, connected to you, endorsed by you, worn by you, or signed by you is going to tell people a lot about you.

Here's a handy list of rules to help you keep a handle on your personal brand:

1. **Exercise strict control over Facebook and other social media content, making full use of any and all privacy settings.** This is an ever-evolving issue, as more and more people sign up and upload more and more personal content onto their Facebook pages and elsewhere. Rule of thumb: if your boss shouldn't see it, don't post it. Period. Because no matter how careful you are, other people aren't. It's social networking, after all. I'm not

going to take you very seriously on Monday morning if you've posted pictures of people doing tequila shots out of your belly button on Saturday night. Also, assume that you can never, ever hide, erase, or abolish anything posted on the Web. Ever.

2. **Dress the part.** Your work clothes are a costume of sorts. They tell people what kind of a businessperson you are. I'm not going to go into specifics—I'm no fashion expert—but I like sharp clothes and sharp dressers. Here's a simple rule of thumb: shop like the Italians. They spend a lot of money on classic staples—suits, shoes, and coats. They're bold and stylish with everything else.

3. **Use extreme caution when signing your name to op-ed articles, letters to the editor, book reviews, and commentaries.** The thumbs-up you gave that anti–global warming book in 1997, the one you no longer agree with in 2012, will linger longer than the ozone layer. That passionate letter to the editor you wrote, criticizing a company you now want to work for—same thing. Google has a permanent memory. If you really must make your opinion heard, use a pseudonym.

4. **Avoid tattoos in places that can't be camouflaged or covered.** I like tattoos. I think some of them are cool. But unless you're opening your own tattoo parlor, or working in an office where you have to step over dogs and around Ping-Pong tables and skateboards to get to your work space, I don't want to know you're a big fan of ancient Sanskrit symbols or Eddie Van Halen or your mom.

5. **Always check the recipient box before hitting Send.** This is self-explanatory. Check and double-check, especially when responding to a particularly testy email. And don't write anything in an email you wouldn't say face to face. Your name is on the email—it can be forwarded, copied, printed, and left around for others to see.

CHAPTER TWELVE

THE O'LEARY FUNDAMENTALS

ANYONE CAN BUILD WEALTH

In the summer of 2008, George and my mother, Georgette, came to Toronto for a visit. Since George's retirement, they had been living in Switzerland, but my mother had had a few health challenges and wanted to come to Canada while she could still get around. After dinner at one of her favorite restaurants, she fell ill. The next day, George called me on the set of *The Lang & O'Leary Exchange* and told me to get to the hospital as fast as possible. My mother had had a heart attack.

We were all at her bedside just before she went for surgery. It should have been routine, but she had a stroke on the operating table, lapsed into a coma, and died a day later. We were all inconsolable.

After the funeral, George told me my mother had made me

the executor of her will. You find out all sorts of things about people after they die. I hadn't realized that my mother was a big collector of some of the finest European couture this side of the pond. It made sense: she had always appreciated good workmanship, having once owned a clothing factory. I also had no idea how much money she had. She married and divorced a salesman who was bad with money, then married a career public servant who made a good living but was by no means rich. They lived well on George's income and traveled widely. My mother often used her own money to help family members, lending money to some — a crucial $10,000 went to me — and fully supporting others through tough times. She was a deeply generous soul, so I expected her savings would have been depleted by the time she died. But there it was in black and white: my mother died with a significant nest egg, one most people could comfortably retire on.

How had she done it? She'd followed a very simple investment plan. Since her days at Kiddies Togs, she had invested a third of her income in bonds and stocks that paid a yield or dividend. By reinvesting that money over the course of sixty or so years, she was able to accumulate a lot. Her savings budget was one to which most people could stick; her investment strategy was easy to understand. She never made a lot of money, but she died having it, because she kept every dime of her principal intact and lived off the interest. It was a revelation. Because I was a student of the markets, I knew that in the last forty years, more than 70 percent of returns had come not from capital appreciation but from dividends. I think my mother must have intuitively known this, which is why she never owned securities that didn't pay interest or a

With my mother in June 2007 in the backyard of our family home in Switzerland.

dividend. I had heard of people investing like this, but when you see the actual results, it's remarkable.

At the same time that I was marveling at my mother's financial wizardry, my own money was taking a major beating. I had invested the cash I'd made in the Mattel deal—wisely, I thought—by leaving half of my earnings with American money managers. The other half I took to Canada, putting two-thirds into stable provincial bonds, which yielded about 6 to 7 percent interest. I put the other third into income trusts, a wholly Canadian asset class that has enjoyed some succulent yields, up to 16 percent. My adviser at the time assured me that the trusts were safe. Plus, the yields were tax-deductible. So I did something entirely uncharacteristic: I moved two-thirds of my money into income trusts, reducing my bond portfolio to one-third. It was a risky move. My mother would have put me in a headlock. She would have driven home the point that the higher the yield, the higher the risk. She would have been right.

On October 2006, the Canadian government slapped a 34 percent tax on income-trust distributions to stem the flow of companies converting to trusts. The government was worried about losing out on significant tax dollars, forgetting how that money was being redistributed in ways the government hadn't even considered. Overnight, income trusts lost about 20 percent of their value, and I lost a significant chunk of my net worth. And let me tell you, I cried like a baby.

FEAR IS YOUR FRIEND

After I wiped my bitter tears, I made appointments with new money managers, telling them about my mother's money, my loss, and my need to feel more secure. I had let greed get in the way of good, sound strategies, and I made a decision to revamp my investment style. I also began to believe that if I felt the need to re-evaluate my investments, other investors must, too. My mother's wealth and its slow, steady incline were based on her commitment to investing only in businesses that could produce yield, so that's what I'd do, too.

I soon discovered my new money managers hadn't been listening to me. One had tied up a significant chunk of my money in Research In Motion (RIM) stock. Nothing wrong with RIM—I love my BlackBerry. But I can't own RIM stock because it doesn't yield any dividends. Another manager had put me in a gold-mining stock in a foreign country, and those stocks plummeted to zero. And I didn't own just 5 percent of the portfolio; the manager had purchased 5 percent of the *entire mine*—with my money!

I could hear my money asking, "Why? Why are you doing this to us?" It was a massive lesson: I hadn't been paying attention to what my money managers were doing, and because those managers hadn't been paying attention to me, they had invested against my style. Most important, they were missing the key component to a healthy investment strategy: fear. The reason you don't put all your money in one place is that you have a healthy fear that your instincts could be wrong. It's a brand of humility, the admission that you might have missed something, or that there are forces at play that you don't understand and cannot know in advance. Fear *must* be part of the investment equation. Without it, you risk being wiped out. But it's hard to incorporate that element when you're not managing your own money. Fear translates into market humility, the ability to stay right-sized, and it can be your friend if tempered with faith in your experience.

After that harrowing financial chapter of my life, I fired those money managers. Then I became my own.

CASH IS KING

In 2008, I gathered my troops together, assessed the damage, and realized that I now had enough money to actually build my own money management firm. From there, perhaps I would attract like-minded investors, those who believed in preservation before appreciation—people like my mother. The entire premise of O'Leary Funds is based on my mother's philosophy of value-yield investing, of only putting money in bonds and stocks that pay a yield or dividend.

I took Georgette's investment philosophy to money managers, trying to find someone who thought like this, who wanted to partner with me to launch this new and exciting series of financial products. I didn't want to find, research, and select the funds myself. That's not my background, training, or forte. I needed a partner who was intellectual, careful, experienced—someone with an eagle eye on protocols and balance sheets. Again, if I was going to grow my wealth, I needed to partner with someone who thought like I thought but carried a completely different skill set from mine.

I found those qualities in Connor O'Brien, an ex–Wall Streeter and Montreal Irishman like me and like my father, Terry. When I brought him my vision—based on capital preservation—he was immediately on board. When I said I no longer wanted to invest in companies that didn't pay a dividend, he agreed. When I said that meant ignoring a whole universe of stocks, no matter how seductive or profitable, he didn't balk. When I said that I didn't care about geography—that this was going to be a truly global

Connor O'Brien (left), CEO of O'Leary Funds, and me—a partnership of the like-minded.

company—he said yes. We both agreed that we wouldn't farm out money to other managers. We'd find experts and hire them. We'd bring them to Montreal, where they'd enjoy significant provincial tax breaks. We'd know their cell numbers, their spouses' names. We'd know where they lived, and when we called them at two in the morning, they'd know where our money was and what it was doing. If we were to visit the office at 5 p.m. on a Thursday, we wanted to see our Asian market specialists at their desks, ready to start their day. Finally, when I said I wouldn't do anything with my money that I couldn't understand, he stood up and shook my hand. We formed a fifty-fifty partnership on the spot. He would select the funds, using his decades of experience with firms such as Merrill Lynch and Lehman Brothers, and I would sell them across the country. We would call our company O'Leary Funds.

Our new strategy was simple. First, we'd strive not to put more than 5 percent of any fund into any one business or venture—even if it was the most exciting idea we'd ever seen. We'd have that discipline. And we'd never put more than 20 percent into a wide sector—like, say, energy. We also looked only for companies that had cash flow. That's all. We wouldn't look at anything else. We said to ourselves that if a company could grow cash, quarter after quarter, two things would likely happen over a thirty-six-month period. One, if we bought bonds and the company continued to increase cash flow, we'd get at least one ratings increase in that period. The upgrade of our bond would then be worth anywhere from 8 to 14 percent in terms of capital appreciation. Two, we'd still be getting yield, upward of another 8 percent. So with that twofold uptick, we could only make money. Over time, by reinvesting the yield, we would grow solid, steady wealth, just as my mother had.

The beauty of our philosophy is that you can't lie about cash; you can't talk about the "vision" of cash. Cash is cash. Either you're making more, or you're not. It's that simple. Anything Georgette would turn her nose up at, we'd reject.

When we took our vision to the banks, they all balked in unison. Investors, they said, want to *grow* money, not just preserve it. We proved them wrong. We're growing at an incredible rate, launching a new fund every three months. With O'Brien, I took a philosophy born out of my mother's style of investing and built a family of funds from zero to $1.5 billion in less than three years.

I view my portfolio like a chicken on a spit—it's got to be dripping cash or something's wrong with the recipe. I realized after starting O'Leary Funds that I had to put my money where my mouth is. After all, I invest in every single fund. It's my money, too, so preservation of capital is number one for me, just as it is for those who entrust me with their money. I look for sustainability of yield and, if and when appropriate, capital appreciation. As I have learned, there are thousands of people who think the same way.

Our average investor at O'Leary Funds is someone in their forties, looking to get serious about building their retirement income. They want steady, realistic, and predictable growth — and a focus on yield, which is precisely what O'Leary Funds tries to give them.

The roller-coaster days of investing are over, and I think a lot of investors feel a healthy caution. I don't think this is a temporary change; I think it's a sea change. It's not enough to assure people their money's being put to work; they want to know it's not being gambled away. Our goal is for O'Leary Funds to hit $5 billion in the next four years. My name launched the funds, but their performance will determine our success. So far, we're doing very well indeed.

SALES IS A FACE-TO-FACE JOB

Technology has made it easier to locate and line up clients and to articulate our trademark message: get paid while you wait. But at the end of the day, I have to put on a suit, get on a plane, and shake some hands. In order to sell our funds, I go on what's called a road show, where I personally cart my own projector and laptop to every pitch meeting. I set everything up myself, test the microphone, loosen my tie, and explain our investment company's simple philosophy. I meet with fund managers in fine restaurants, and everyday investors in rented movie theaters. It's an unrelenting schedule—some weeks, I am on a plane twice a day, making my way across the country and back. But far from finding it onerous, I thrive on the road. It's bred in my bones, after all.

Whenever I snap open my briefcase and hand out our prospectuses, I think of my forebears. I think of my Lebanese grandfather, Joseph Bookalam, who went door to door as a teenager, selling hunting and fishing supplies until he made enough money to start his kids' clothing business in Montreal. I think of my father, Terry O'Leary, who came over on a boat from Ireland to sell winter coats and hats made in my grandfather's factory. I think of holding the hand of my stepfather, George, as he visited rural fishing outposts in Cambodia and modernized factories in Cyprus, intently dispensing advice that would help make them more profitable. And I think of my wonderful mother, Georgette, who knew that money was important only because it gave you the ultimate gift: freedom.

I also think of the great partners I've had in all my business ventures—from Paul Chaput, my shuffleboard mate, to the guys from Special Event Television, Scott MacKenzie and Dave Toms. I think of the SoftKey crew, including John Freeman and, of course, Michael Perik, Scott Murray, and Tony Bordon. I also think of Reza Satchu, and how we went on to sell Storage Now for more than $100 million. And I think of my current partner, Connor O'Brien, a masterful money manager who complements my ability to get out there and sell our funds. By the way, no one's ever done what we've done, raising $1.5 billion in less than three years. And we did it during one of the worst economic downturns in recent history.

THERE IS NO SUCH THING AS A TRULY LOCAL ECONOMY

I could, and probably will, write a whole book specifically on where to put your money and how to invest to grow, but here's a broad outline of my favorite opportunities. I like growth markets, because I like to invest in sectors from which I don't have to steal market share, where I can just be part of the wave that's already intact and moving forward. Chief among these trends today is infrastructure spending.

Building, repairing, updating, and retrofitting bridges, airports, roads, and rail lines—these are projects usually undertaken by governments and executed by private contractors using local raw materials. Just consider your commute home—every road-construction detour, every overpass repair and airport extension project. These are all government contracts that go to the lowest bidder and are the kinds of companies I love to invest in. If I was left with any lasting legacy from my peripatetic childhood, it is that infrastructure spending is a constant around the world, somewhere in the trillions. Everywhere my family traveled, a massive government infrastructure project was under way. Almost fifty years later, the world's no different. In fact, in the wake of the most recent economic meltdown, infrastructure spending seems to be on the tongues of global leaders looking to leverage their countries out of debt and joblessness. "Jobs, jobs, jobs" is the new mantra. And when governments tell me they are going to spend billions investing in infrastructure to create those jobs, I believe them. Because if there is one thing governments everywhere in the world know how to do well, it's spend money.

So much is made of the emerging monoliths of China and India. And for good reason. There's no arguing that they're both eclipsing the North American markets when it comes to manufacturing, spending, and growth. In fact, for the first time in history, there are more billion-dollar companies outside of North America than in it. And I do invest heavily in both India and China. But the market I keep the keenest eye on is Brazil. It's a big, vibrant, educated, and stable country. It hasn't been involved in any kind of international conflict in generations, because Brazil's interested in making money (and love), not war, and I like that. It's a country of almost two hundred million people who all want the things you already have.

If I were just starting out, fresh out of an MBA program, I'd buy a one-way ticket to São Paulo, get off the plane, and figure out how to get rich off that appetite for consumer goods. You can't build a riper, hungrier market than Brazil. O'Leary Funds is a long-term investor in one of the largest hydroelectric plants in Brazil. Demand will increase over the next twenty-five years, and I'm counting on an 8 to 10 percent yield. We're also investing in Brazilian telecommunications companies, pipelines, ports, and roadways. We own a little bit of everything in that country, because, in a couple of decades, I believe Brazil's output will eclipse the GNP of North America.

O'LEARY'S LAWS FOR
SAVVY INVESTING

1. **Know the news.** Watch, read, or stream a reliable source. I like to get my business news from *The Wall Street Journal*, the *Bloomberg Report*, *The New York Times*, and *The Economist*. I get them all on my iPad so I can refresh information on the go. I also keep one eye on every TV screen in every airport I pass through. So many people think they just have to keep their eyes on financial institutions and markets, forgetting that elections, natural disasters, revolutions—even royal weddings—can change a country's fortunes in an instant. If you want to be a successful investor, you must remain alert, curious, and in touch with what's happening in the world on every level. But beyond current events, pay attention to history. As I mentioned, in the past forty years, more than 70 percent of all returns came from dividends, not capital appreciation. So you should never own anything that doesn't pay a yield.

2. **Get over your fear of globalization.** It's here to stay—and for my money (quite literally), globalization does far more good than harm. The rising standard of living in countries like India, China, and Brazil means more money, more jobs, more education, and most important, more freedom. And as an investor, I want to ride that bandwagon into new and bursting economies. Besides, international investing opportunities offer some of the best yields you can find.

3. **Pay attention to the signs.** No matter what kind of traveling you're doing, whether for business or pleasure, keep your eyes peeled for valuable hints about how the economy's going. How modern is the airport? What are the road conditions? If you're traveling in a developing country, do salt, soap, sugar, and other commodities abound, or are they scarce? You want to know how the average Joe in Jakarta is faring, because the happier he is, the more he's spending, and the more he's spending, the faster his economy is going to grow. I like catching a country on the upswing.

4. **Learn another language.** I regret that I didn't learn French when I had the chance. But while learning a new language from scratch is out of the question right now, I make up for it by throwing myself into a country's culture enthusiastically. I eat the local cuisine, listen to local music, learn the history and idioms. It helps me to think locally about the country in which I'm contemplating investing. If I think like the locals and spend like the locals, I can see the country's economy through their eyes. That gives me a cool advantage as an investor. I can react to opportunities on a visceral, not just an intellectual, level.

5. **Where's your money?** Here's the thing about a global economy: you probably already *are* an international investor. Many Canadian companies aren't Canadian at all. Canadian Pacific Hotels are owned by companies based in Saudi Arabia and California; Stelco was taken over by U.S. Steel in 2007; and the venerable Molson brewery merged with Colorado-based Coors

back in 2005. Even CCM, the company that made my first pair of skates, is owned by Reebok. So if you have a gripe about investing beyond your borders, get over it. Smarter investors already have.

FULL CIRCLE

ENTREPRENEURS ARE CAPITALISM'S SUPERHEROES

It was December 2010. I was in the Back Bay neighborhood of Boston, hurrying to meet a TV crew from *Shark Tank*. Remember Marc Furigay, the Chicago teacher who started a business putting Shakespeare to rap music? All five Sharks were in, but I had to run the idea past an expert in educational publishing, Tony Bordon. You may remember Tony as my vice-president in charge of retail back in the days of SoftKey and TLC. Believe it or not, Tony is still with The Learning Company—a newly revamped version of the company, which was acquired by the venerable publishing giant Houghton Mifflin.

I was meeting with Tony just days after TLC had announced a new line of mobile applications and Facebook games featuring three of its most beloved brands: Reader Rabbit, Oregon Trail, and Carmen Sandiego. The announcement was among the most popular topics on Twitter, striking a nostalgic chord with a generation of young parents who grew up with those beloved characters. Taking the elevator up to TLC's suite of offices to meet Tony, I thought back to when Mattel blamed TLC's "tired" brands for its demise. Today, TLC is a shiny new entity on the cusp of a massive rebirth.

Shaking Tony's hand in the TLC boardroom that morning, I had the sense that everything in my life had come full circle. TLC was up and running again, and I was feeding new ideas its way. I thought back to the non-compete clause that had prevented me from working in the educational software industry for years. Were it not for that clause, I would never have pursued TV work. And were it not for TV work, I would not have been there with Tony that morning, doing business, making deals, and earning money. I introduced Tony to Marc and watched him pitch his idea to license his Shakespearean rap songs to TLC. I stood back and watched the cameras capture the moment when a possibility becomes an opportunity—when a creator finally gets to meet a believer.

Entrepreneurs do something governments can't do: we inspire the next generation of wealth builders. The pursuit of wealth is fascinating to watch. Shows like *Dragons' Den* and *Shark Tank* demonstrate again and again the power of money and the freedom it affords. When money flows toward a good idea, everyone feels it—the venture capitalists, the entrepreneurs, the viewers and the consumer. That's the power of money.

FREEDOM IS THE ONLY THING MONEY
TRULY BUYS YOU

Recently, while sitting at my desk in my Muskoka country home, which overlooks Lake Joseph, I thought of that guy who called me an asshole in the airport washroom a few years ago. I was organizing the next few months of my life. *Dragons' Den* was gearing up to shoot season six, and we had just wrapped the second season of *Shark Tank*. O'Leary Funds was outperforming our projections. Then there were my various board commitments, speaking engagements, and fundraising ventures, not to mention a bit of fun scheduled with friends and family. Every single commitment in my

calendar was a choice. I didn't *need* to do any of those things, but I *wanted* to do all of them. For a moment, I let it sink in: I'd never been busier, happier, wealthier, or freer.

I hope this book empowers you to pursue that kind of freedom—for yourself and for others. I hope it touches a few readers with that same force of life. Freedom is a gift I'm grateful for every day. It is the result not of being an asshole, but of a single-minded pursuit of the only thing that matters in business: money. I took great risks and made some hefty sacrifices to get here, and I'll do whatever it takes to stay here. Because let me tell you, *here* is a very nice place.

We built this Muskoka home from scratch, about the only extravagance I've never regretted. I can hear the loons in the nearby inlets, and I can see the spectacular color change that happens every fall. A few friends are coming over for a casual get-together. I'll select a fine bottle of Burgundy, capping it off with a rare port, chosen from a wine cellar that's carved out of the Canadian Shield. After dinner, everyone will gather around a fire near the dock, and we'll lift our glasses to toast—not to wealth, not to success, not even to money—but to freedom.

ACKNOWLEDGEMENTS

Everybody has a story; this book is mine. I had no idea when I began this project that telling the story of my life would be so cathartic. Going all the way back to the touch points of my early childhood was both exhilarating and painful. And scrutinizing my own career with 20/20 hindsight has made me realize just how much my success is really a mysterious combination of hard work and plain-old serendipity. Because in the end, fortune shines on only a lucky few and sets them free.

I feel a lot of gratitude when I think back to the hundreds of people I have met and worked with over the years. Some remain close friends and others have faded into distant memory, but all were an important part of my journey. Chief among them were my business partners and colleagues, including John Freeman, Gary Babcock and Mary Pat Lyons, who helped start all of this; Jerry Patterson, who gave me those early lessons; Dave Toms, Scott MacKenzie, Don Cherry, and Don Allen (who offered that "first office"). Gratitude to Michael Perik, Scott Murray, Dave Patrick, Sanjay Khosla, Tony Bordon and the incredibly talented management team at SoftKey Software Products and The

Learning Company for going on a wild ride with me. That ride was fueled by the billions of investment dollars we raised with bankers such as Owen Mitchell, Gene McBurney, Scott Patterson, Thomas H. Lee, Scott Sperling, Tony DiNovi, and Mark Nunley. Thank you all.

Much thanks also to Reza Satchu for helping me land on my feet and to Connor O'Brien, Louise Anne Poirier and the fifty highly skilled money managers and professionals from around the world who have not only helped me break new ground by building O'Leary Funds from scratch but have also raised billions of dollars. Special mention goes to Anita Bell, who in addition to her role syndicating O'Leary Funds also syndicates my time — a very challenging task at which she excels. And much thanks to Alex Kenjeev, who runs my legal affairs and keeps me on the right side of the law!

To my TV compatriots, a big thank you goes out to Jasper James, Mark Burnett, Stuart Coxe, Tracie Tighe, Julie Bristow, Kristine Stewart, Dianne Buckner and the rest of the crew at *Dragons' Den* and *Shark Tank*, and to all my fellow financial Shark and Dragon carnivores — Arlene Dickinson, Robert Herjavec, Brett Wilson, Jim Treliving, Laurence Lewin (I really miss him), Daymond John, Barbara Corcoran, Kevin Harrington, Mark Cuban, and Jeff Foxworthy. If there were ever a battle between the Dragons and Sharks, it would probably be a tie. Shout out to everyone at *The Lang & O'Leary Exchange*, notably Amanda Lang, the best TV wife a guy could ask for. And I especially want to thank Lisa Gabriele, who helped me take my thoughts, ideas, stories, opinions, memories and experiences and put them together in this book — all while show-running

Dragons' Den. She is truly an artist with remarkable talent. I'd also like to thank the folks at Doubleday, Nita Pronovost, Brad Martin and Kristin Cochrane, for their enthusiasm and support for this book.

Finally, thank you to Linda and my children, Savannah and Trevor, who continue to motivate me to succeed. Love and gratitude to my late father, Terry O'Leary, and to my first partner in life, my brother, Shane O'Leary. Thanks to my cousin, Michael Bookalam, Suzanne and Elaine Aboud, and Lynn Bookalam for filling in some family history. Mostly, I want to thank my beloved stepfather, George Kanawaty. Without his careful reads and timely, thoughtful edits—not to mention his steel-trap memory—I could never have produced such a thorough account of my life and my work. I also want to thank him for being such an incredible mentor, advisor, parent, and husband to my mother, Georgette. We all miss her so much, and I hope her wise and loving spirit can be felt on every page of this book.